Cicero's Consulship Campaign

Second Edition

LACTOR Sourcebooks in Ancient History

For more than half a century, *LACTOR Sourcebooks in Ancient History* have been providing for the needs of students at schools and universities who are studying ancient history in English translation. Each volume focuses on a particular period or topic and offers a generous and judicious selection of primary texts in new translations. The texts selected include not only extracts from important literary sources but also numerous inscriptions, coin legends and extracts from legal and other texts, which are not otherwise easy for students to access. Many volumes include annotation as well as a glossary, maps and other relevant illustrations, and sometimes a short Introduction. The volumes are written and reviewed by experienced teachers of ancient history at both schools and universities. The series is now being published in print and digital form by Cambridge University Press, with plans for both new editions and completely new volumes.

Osborne	*The Athenian Empire*
Osborne	*The Old Oligarch*
Cooley	*Cicero's Consulship Campaign*
Grocock	*Inscriptions of Roman Britain*
Osborne	*Athenian Democracy*
Santangelo	*Late Republican Rome, 88-31 BC*
Warmington/Miller	*Inscriptions of the Roman Empire, AD 14-117*
Treggiari	*Cicero's Cilician Letters*
Rathbone/Rathbone	*Literary Sources for Roman Britain*
Sabben-Clare/Warman	*The Culture of Athens*
Stockton	*From the Gracchi to Sulla*
Edmondson	*Dio: the Julio-Claudians*
Brosius	*The Persian Empire from Cyrus II to Artaxerxes I*
Cooley/Wilson	*The Age of Augustus*
Levick	*The High Tide of Empire*
Cooley	*Tiberius to Nero*
Cooley	*The Flavians*
Cooley	*Sparta*

Cicero's Consulship Campaign

A selection of sources relating to Cicero's election as consul for 63BC, including 'A Short Guide to Electioneering'

Second Edition

———

Introduction and notes by
M. G. L. COOLEY
Warwick School

Translations by
M. G. L. COOLEY, J. MURRELL, D. W. TAYLOR,
M. A. THORPE

 CAMBRIDGE
UNIVERSITY PRESS

Shaftesbury Road, Cambridge CB2 8EA, United Kingdom

One Liberty Plaza, 20th Floor, New York, NY 10006, USA

477 Williamstown Road, Port Melbourne, VIC 3207, Australia

314–321, 3rd Floor, Plot 3, Splendor Forum, Jasola District Centre, New Delhi – 110025, India

103 Penang Road, #05–06/07, Visioncrest Commercial, Singapore 238467

Cambridge University Press is part of Cambridge University Press & Assessment, a department of the University of Cambridge.

We share the University's mission to contribute to society through the pursuit of education, learning and research at the highest international levels of excellence.

www.cambridge.org
Information on this title: www.cambridge.org/9781009383523
DOI: 10.1017/9781009383547

First published 2023

A catalogue record for this publication is available from the British Library.

A Cataloging-in-Publication data record for this book is available from the Library of Congress.

ISBN 978-1-009-38352-3 Paperback

TABLE OF CONTENTS

INTRODUCTION AND ACKNOWLEDGEMENTS

The first version of LACTOR 3, *A Short Guide to Electioneering* was published just over 40 years ago, one of the first of the series. 40 years later, Ancient History has survived the most recent threat to its existence as a discrete A-level, thanks to the highly-publicised togate appearance of Boris Johnson, soon to win the London mayoral election, and the less visible, but equally vital work of many professional and amateur (in the word's truest sense) classicists. The translation, by D.W. Taylor and John Murrell is once again on the syllabus of a Cicero topic, hence the most pressing reason for a reprint of this text. But much has changed too, and the LACTOR committee feels that LACTOR volumes should provide greater help in the form of notes on the text.

Forty years have not solved the question of authorship of the *commentariolum*, though there now seems to be general agreement that it is a very important and informative document for studying the politics of the late Roman republic.

The new volume also includes texts which cast further light on the elections for 63 BC: two letters from Cicero to his great friend Atticus show the campaign beginning over a year before the polls. During the campaign proper, Cicero made a public speech against the election pact of his two main rivals. This does not survive, but a commentary by the Roman scholar Asconius does. Right at the start of his year in office, Cicero delivered a speech on a land-reform bill proposed by one of the new tribunes in which he reflects on his election. Finally, Cicero's *pro Murena* delivered when he was consul, defending one of the consuls elected for the following year against a charge of election bribery, gives us a very different angle on the elections of the time. Sections 21–25 of this speech (in the currently prescribed text) are reproduced from LACTOR 7: translations of the other parts of this speech are mine. The volume deliberately omits, however, the main events of 63 BC, relating to the Catilinarian conspiracy, and also Cicero's many reflections on his consulship.

It is a pleasure to thank those whose work on previous LACTOR volumes is here reissued. I hope they will feel that my efforts do justice to theirs. If so, this will be in no small part due to the help offered by Jeffrey Tatum, and the improvements suggested by Catherine Steel and Dominic Rathbone. My greatest debt is to my wife, Alison, whose careful reading has saved me from many errors, great and small. This book is for our son, Paul.

M.G.L. Cooley
General Editor of LACTOR
Warwick School
April 2009

GLOSSARY

amicus, *pl.* **amici**
SGE 3, 5, 8, 14, 16, 18, 20, 28, 29, 31, 32, 33, 35, 39, 40, 44, 46, 49
Atticus 1.1.1, 1.1.2, 1.1.4; Asconius 2; *Murena* 42, 43, 45
Sometimes a friend or acquaintance (Latin has two words, *familiaris* and *necessarius*, to describe a close friend), sometimes a political ally, usually a mixture (perhaps best translated as 'associate'). Roman politics had no political parties and was so small in scale that most political groups were transient and based on the mutual interests and/ or liking of a few men.

amicitia, *pl.* **amicitiae**
SGE 23, 25, 26, 27, 29, 30, 31, 32, 33, 39, 40, 41; *Murena* 24
The relationship between *amici*. A letter of Cicero to Pompey in December 62, (Cic., *Letter To Friends* 5.7 = SB F3) refers to *amicitia* between them, where mutual self-interest, rather than personal affection or long-term political alliance is meant.
    See: *SGE* 16 and 25–7, distinguishing between *amicitia* in 'normal' life and in an election campaign; P.A. Brunt, *The Fall of the Roman Republic*, chapter 7; A. Lintott, *The Constitution of the Roman Republic*, pages 170–3.

centuria, *pl.* **centuriae**
SGE 18, 29, 32, 33, 56; Asconius 5, epilogue
Centuriae were voting-groups at the assembly of the people (*comitia centuriata*) which elected consuls and praetors and passed legislation. Membership of the 193 *centuriae* depended on property-qualifications. After one *centuria* selected by lot, 70 *centuriae* of the first (richest) class voted first, followed by 18 *centuriae equitum* (equestrians).
    See: Cicero, *Philippics* 2.82; *CAH* vii.2² pages 198–204, 337–338, 440–443; Lintott, *Constitution*, pages 55–61.

collegium, *pl.* **collegia**
SGE 3, 16, 19, 30, 32
In general any group of at least three men with a common purpose; these might be trade-guilds, cults, clubs. These were convenient centres of political support, since they all possessed a degree of organisation, capable of mobilising support.
    See: Lintott, *Constitution*, pages 177–8.

consul, *pl.* **consuls**
Atticus 1.1.2; 1.2.1; *SGE* 18; Asconius 13, 15, epilogue; *Agrarian law* 3, 4, 6; *Murena* 24, 38, 42
The two heads of state, elected annually by the people. Candidates had to have served as *praetors* three or more years previously. Their wide-ranging civil and military powers were limited by the one-year period of office and the presence of a colleague with the same powers.
    See: Lintott, *Constitution*, pages 104–7.

eques, *pl.* **equites**
SGE 3, 9, 10, 13, 29, 33, 50, 53, 55; Asconius, (pref), 8, 16, (17)
In a narrow sense, 1,800 members of the 18 equestrian *centuriae*. More often in the late Republic, a wider sense is meant, including all freeborn male citizens who possessed property worth more than 400,000 sesterces. In this sense they were not a coherent, self-conscious group: some were rich farmers, some traders and money-lenders, others *publicani* (tax-farmers), and their interests were not identical. They are often mentioned here, since to a *novus homo*, born an *eques*, their support was valuable: a *nobilis* would be likely to rely on family connections within the senatorial order for his support.
    See: P.A. Brunt, *The Fall of the Roman Republic*, chapter 3, "The *Equites*"; *CAH* ix², pages 90–2.

nobilis, *pl.* **nobiles**
Atticus 1.1.2, 1.2.2; *SGE* 4, 50; Asconius. pref, 1, 26; *Agrarian law* 3; *Murena* 24
The aristocracy who ruled the Republic. A man who reached the consulship made all his descendants *nobiles*. This office was therefore the entrance to the ruling elite for a *novus homo*. In Cicero's day, 90% of consuls were *nobiles*.
    See: Lintott, *Constitution*, pages 164–170; "*Nobilitas*" in *OCD*.

novus homo, *pl.* **novi homines**
SGE 2, 3, 4, 7, 11, 13, 14, 54; *Agrarian Law* 3, 4,
This term could apply to someone, none of whose direct ancestors had been a senator, or to someone, none of whose direct ancestors had been consul (though they might still have been in the Senate), or to someone, like Cicero, who made it to the consulship, despite having no direct ancestors in the Senate.
    See: T.P. Wiseman, *New Men in the Roman Senate*; "novus homo" in *OCD*.

optimates
SGE 5; Asconius 25
Those who wished to preserve the status quo, in particular the predominance of the Senate; also used to refer to the leading men of this view in the Senate. Like the *populares*, they were in no sense an organised political party.
    See: *CAH* ix², pages 48–53; Lintott, *Constitution*, pages 173–4.

popularis, *pl.* **populares**
SGE 5, 53; Asconius 2, 9; *Agrarian Law* 6, 7
Adjective, used in the plural as a noun, to describe politicians (usually *nobiles* and senators) who legislated for the interests of the people (*populus*), using popular assemblies rather than the Senate. They were regarded as dangerous radicals by the *optimates*, though probably in reality both groups aimed at personal power and prestige, differing only in their methods.
    See: Lintott, *Constitution*, pages 173–6 and 205–8; Wiseman, *Remembering the Roman People*, ch. 1, for the opposite view, that there really was an ideological split between *popularis* and optimate.

praetors

SGE 8, 13; Asconius 2, 3, 4, 5, 12, 24, 26; *Agrarian law* 3; *Murena* 37, 41, 42

Magistrates next in importance to consuls: eight elected annually by popular assembly from candidates who had previously held a more junior magistracy. Their principal duty was to preside over the courts set up by Sulla. The great majority would then govern a province in the year following their praetorship. See note on page 45.

See: Lintott, *Constitution*, pages 107–9; *"praetor – Republic"* in *OCD*.

tribunus plebis, *pl.* **tribuni plebis**

Atticus 1.1.1; *SGE* 18; Asconius pref, 2, 5, 13; *Murena* 24

The *tribuni plebis* or tribunes of the people were ten annually elected officers armed with negative and obstructive powers designed to protect the *plebs* from victimisation by magistrates. A tribune could intercede on behalf of an individual, arrest any magistrate and veto assemblies and any decision of the Senate. Tribunes were the main proposers of legislation in the later Republic and the tribunate became the typical office of a *popularis* politician.

See Lintott, *Constitution* 121–128.

Two Letters Of Cicero To Atticus

Titus Pomponius Atticus (110–32 BC) was one of the best-known and wealthiest figures of the late republic. He shunned political office and chose to spend much of his life in Athens, though being friend to prominent politicians of every opinion. An especially close friend to Cicero from their schooldays (Atticus' sister married Cicero's brother, Quintus), Atticus was a writer himself, and Cicero's literary adviser.

These letters are to be taken, in comparison with his speeches, as a more sincere representation of his opinions – expressed to an intimate friend of over 30 years' standing, and without any thought for publication. Atticus did however have a very wide circle of friends and though Cicero is joking in asking Atticus to tell Pompey not to come to his election (below, 1.1.2) he clearly hoped Atticus could be influential in winning or preserving the support of others (below, 1.1.3–4; 1.2.2).

In the first letter, dated 17 July, 65 BC, Cicero can be seen sizing up his likely election rivals for the consulship of 63 BC over a year before elections. Any candidate would be able to gather quite a good idea of his rivals since Sulla's recent legislation as dictator had regulated the steps of a political career. A potential consul now had to have been quaestor and praetor, and there were minimum age requirements for each post as well as mandatory gaps between office. The most ambitious and successful politicians would tend to stand and be elected as soon as eligible. Cicero achieved this in his election as quaestor in 75 (thus entering the Senate), and praetor in 66. He would be eligible for the final step, the consulship, in 63, along with others from 'his own year-group'. As he is well aware, his big advantage is his fame as an advocate, his big disadvantage is his status as a *novus homo* ('new man' – see glossary, page 6).

The real reason, however, for Cicero writing to Atticus is to apologise for having potentially offended two rich and prominent close connections of Atticus in circumstances which he connects to his candidacy.

Cicero, *Letters to Atticus* 1.1 = Shackleton Bailey 10

Written at Rome, shortly before 17 July 65
Cicero to Atticus, greetings.

[1] Regarding my election campaign, which I know is of great interest to you, the situation, as far as one can guess at present, is this: Publius Galba alone is campaigning. He is meeting a plain, unvarnished, old-fashioned, "no". The word on the street is that this premature canvass of his has done my prospects no harm. For people generally are refusing to support him because they say they owe me their support. So I hope to derive some advantage when it becomes generally known that very many of my *amici* are coming forward. I was actually thinking of starting my campaign at the same time as Cincius says your slave will set off with this letter, that is on 17 July, at the elections for tribunes in the Field of Mars. My rivals who seem certain to stand are Galba, Antonius and – I think this will make you laugh or cry – Quintus Cornificius. You will scratch your head at the news that some think Caesonius will join the list. Aquilius, I think, is unlikely to: he has stated he will not, has entered a plea of ill-health, and has offered his judicial dominion as an excuse. Catiline will certainly stand if the jury in his case adjudges that it's dark at midday. As for Aufidius and Palicanus, I don't think you are holding your breath for news from me.

[2] On those who are seeking election this time, Caesar is thought a certainty. Thermus and Silanus are thought to be contesting the other place. They are so short of *amici* or reputation that in my opinion it's not impossible for Turius to overtake them; but no one else seems to agree. It would be greatly to my advantage for Thermus to make it together with Caesar, since none of the current candidates would seem to be as strong a candidate if left over to my year, especially given that he is Curator of the Flaminian Way which will then be finished, no question. I would happily now stick him in with the consul Caesar. This is my current way of thinking of the candidates. I shall apply myself to the best of my ability in fulfilling every requirement of a candidate. Perhaps, since Northern Italy looks very important in determining the result, when the courts at Rome are in recess, I shall run down in September to assist Piso and return in January. When I have investigated the preferences of the *nobiles* I shall write to you. I hope the rest is going well, at least as regards my rivals in the city. Since you are closer at hand, make sure you answer for the other group, that of our *amicus*, Pompey. Say that I won't mind if he doesn't come for my election.

[1] Publius Sulpicius **Galba** was in many respects Cicero's exact opposite, apparently of no real substance as a person or politician, but from a very distinguished family indeed. He is mentioned dismissively by Q. Cicero and Asconius. Of his other election rivals, what Cicero says here about Quintus **Cornificius**, **Caesonius**, **Aquilius**, **Aufidius** and **Palicanus**, is more or less self-explanatory: of these only Cornificius actually stood. Cicero's two most serious rivals were Gaius **Antonius** and Lucius Sergius Catilina. The latter, usually known in English as **Catiline**, and later the conspirator, was then facing trial for extortion, but was acquitted. **Cincius** was an agent of Atticus, frequently mentioned in Cicero's letters to Atticus.

[2] Cicero was also clearly keeping a close eye on elections that summer, since a defeated candidate could well stand again for the following year. This **Caesar** is not the famous dictator, but Lucius Julius Caesar. His father and the aunt of Julius Caesar the *dictator* were cousins. He was duly elected as consul. His colleague as consul was Gaius Marcius Figulus. This must have been **Thermus**, legally adopted into a new family – a process very common in Rome for reasons of social and political prestige. A 'Turius' is later mentioned by Cicero (*Brutus* 237) as once having come within a few voting centuries of a consulship. **Silanus** missed out in the election for 64 but was elected for 62.

Cicero shows that votes of citizens living outside Rome could be important. After the Social War (91–87 BC), most areas of Italy had full citizen rights, though voting in elections entailed travel to Rome. The **Curator of the Flaminian Way**, which ran 209 miles north from Rome to Rimini was responsible for awarding considerable contracts and opportunities for employment and could thus gain popularity, as did Julius Caesar (Plutarch, *Caesar* 5.5). **Northern Italy**: the area of modern Italy between the Northern Apennines and the River Po. This area, which the Romans called Gallia Cispadana had been fully enfranchised in 80. Gaius Calpurnius **Piso** (consul 67), a leading *nobilis*, was governor of the area beyond the Po. Gnaeus Pompeius Magnus – **Pompey** the Great was the most prominent politician and general of the day. From 66 he was in Asia (Turkey) campaigning successfully against Rome's chief enemy Mithridates, so **closer at hand** to Atticus in Greece. Cicero **won't mind** if Pompey does not return for his election (though he is joking in asking Atticus to say so). The comment shows that there is no *amicitia* between the two and Cicero fears Pompey will oppose his election if Pompey is in Rome.

(The letter continues ...)

[3] So that's how things are. But there is something for which I have to beg your pardon. Caecilius, your uncle, was defrauded of a great deal of money by Publius Varius. He has begun a lawsuit against Varius' brother, Caninius Satyrus for items which he is said to have received fraudulently from Varius. Other creditors, including Lucullus and Publius Scipio, are acting with him, as is Lucius Pontius who people think will be responsible for auctioning off Satyrus' goods if he goes bankrupt – but such an idea is ridiculous. To come to the point. Your uncle has asked me to represent him against

Satyrus. Not a day passes without Satyrus calling on me: he looks to Lucius Domitius first, but to me next. He was very useful both to Quintus and to me in our campaigns.

[4] Of course I am in a very difficult position because of my close friendship to Satyrus himself and to Domitius, the one man on whom my candidature particularly depends. I pointed this out to Caecilius, while explaining that had the case involved only him and Satyrus, I would have obliged him. As it was, the situation involved many creditors, men of the highest rank. They could easily maintain their joint legal action without Caecilius having anyone acting specifically for him. It would, I suggested, be right for him to make allowance for my obligations and current situation. He seemed to me to take this less well than I had hoped, or than a gentleman should, and from then on he completely shunned the friendly relations which we had recently established.

Please forgive me for this and be assured that I could not in all decency appear against an *amicus* in his worst hour and when his whole reputation was at stake, when he had previously given me every support in word and deed. Or to take a more negative view of me, you may assume that my campaign prevented me. But even if you take this view, I should be forgiven since it's a matter of life and death. You see the path we are on, and how important we think it is not only to maintain supporters but also acquire new ones. I hope you now agree with my side of the case – I very much want you to.

[5] I really love your statue of Hermes and Athena. It is so splendidly placed that the whole hall seems like an offering to it. With very best wishes.

[3] Cornelius Nepos, an acquaintance of both Cicero and Atticus, and biographer of the latter, provides some background. 'Atticus had an uncle, Quintus **Caecilius**, a Roman *eques* and close friend of Lucius **Lucullus**. Caecilius was rich and very difficult in character, but Atticus, although no one else could bear him, humoured his ill-temper, retaining his goodwill and not giving him any cause for offence even when he was very old.' (Nepos, *Atticus* 5.1). **Lucullus** (*c.* 118–56 BC) was also one of Rome's most prominent politicians and generals, though by 65 BC, his power and influence was very much on the wane (see notes on page 46). **Scipio** was a young man from one of Rome's most famous families. None of **Varius**, **Satyrus** and **Pontius** is prominent.

[4] Lucius **Domitius** Ahenobarbus was born in 98 BC. In 70, Cicero had described him five years before as 'a young man from the most noble of families and leader of the younger generation' (*Speech against Verres* II.1.139). In fact his great-great-grandfather, great-grandfather, grandfather and father had all reached the consulship, as did he in 54 BC, and four generations of his descendants. The support of this young aristocrat was of great importance: to avoid offending Domitius by prosecuting his client, Satyrus, Cicero rather improperly evaded his own patronal obligation to Caecilius and Atticus, even at the risk of offending both them and Lucullus. This part of the letter well illustrates several of the topics mentioned in Quintus Cicero's 'Short Guide to Electioneering' and the 'slippery slope' faced by most politicians, but especially ones relying on a network of personal support (*amicitia*) in the absence of any political parties. It also shows how carefully we must read Cicero: Lintott notes that 'The letter is presented as a progress report, but for both writer and recipient the request made in the latter part of the letter was the nub … Atticus is not only expected to forgive Cicero himself, but to see that Lucullus and his friends forgive him also.' *Cicero as Evidence*, page 5.

Cicero, *Letters to Atticus* 1.2 = Shackleton Bailey 11

Written at Rome, shortly after 17 July 65
Cicero to Atticus, greetings.

[1] On the day on which Lucius Julius Caesar and Gaius Marcius Figulus were elected consuls, I am blessed with a little boy. Terentia is doing well. I have not heard from you for a long time. I wrote to you in detail earlier about my position. At this moment I am thinking of defending Catiline, my fellow-candidate. We have the jurors we want, with the full agreement of the prosecutor. I hope if he is acquitted he will be more closely associated with me in the matter of campaigning; if it turns out otherwise, I shall grin and bear it.

[2] I need your early return home. For there is a distinctly widespread feeling among people that your friends, the *nobiles*, will oppose my election. I can see that you will be of the greatest benefit to me in winning over their support for me. So do see that you are in Rome at the beginning of January, as arranged.

This letter gives us the fascinating information, hardly to be guessed from the previous letter or subsequent speeches, that Cicero seriously considered the defence of **Catiline** on the charge of extortion. In fact the comment about the jury indicates that the jury had already been selected. As is clear from Cicero's prosecution of Verres, prosecution and defence could reject potential jurors (Cicero, *Verrines* 2.17–19).Yet Cicero withdrew at a late stage as Asconius rightly deduces from Cicero making no reference to having helped Catiline (see below, Asconius [4–5]). The prosecutor was P. Clodius Pulcher (see footnote 76).

'A SHORT GUIDE TO ELECTIONEERING'
(?) QUINTUS CICERO, *COMMENTARIOLUM PETITIONIS*

This pamphlet which calls itself *commentariolum petitionis* or 'a short guide to electioneering' was allegedly written by Quintus Cicero, younger brother of Marcus to his elder brother during his campaign for the consulship of 63 BC. There has long been debate about whether the document is really by Quintus Cicero or whether its origin was in the sort of imitative literary exercise widely practised in Rome during the imperial period. The prevalent view now is that the work is genuine, written by Quintus possibly with the intention that a limited circulation of copies could help his brother's campaign.

Certainly the work presents a very favourable impression of Marcus Cicero, both as a person, and as a serious candidate for the consulship. His various good qualities are repeatedly stressed, right from the very first sentence. Obviously his oratory is given pride of place (2) with particular stress placed on those who have benefited from his advocacy (19–21, 38, 51). Cicero's personal qualities are much in evidence, whether presented implicitly (attention, diligence and hard work – 3, 15); through contrast with rivals (7–10, 28); or through evidence of his high moral standards: as in a skilful reference, the writer admits to such faults in his subject as may well be read as positive virtues (too trusting – 39; lacks flattery – 41; too honest as a disciple of Plato – 45–8).

As regards his candidacy, Cicero's skill as campaigner is obvious at the start and end of the work with the writer of the guide (who had by 64 BC won election as quaestor and aedile) deferring to Marcus Cicero's greater expertise (1 and 58). The reader is made to feel that Cicero is already doing in practice most of the things being recommended in theory, and more ('take care to hold on to these advantages ...' – 4; 'young men of noble birth ... you have very many of them' – 6; 'I know full well that you are aware...' – 14; *amicitiae* that have been gained and confirmed already' – 25; 'secure your strength in each *centuria*...' – 29; 'recognition of men: see that you show this quite clearly ...' – 42; 'You have already gained the support of the city crowds – 51; 'keep to the path you have started on' – 55;) and the impressive scale and range of his existing supporters is often stressed (3, 6, 14, 19–22, 38, 50, 51). All in all the impression is given that only immoral or illegal behaviour by others could prevent his success (1 – fraud; 13 – envy; 39 – treachery; 54- evils of Rome; 55, 57 – bribery).

For further discussion, see (with full references in bibliography) Morstein-Marx, Tatum (*Phoenix* 2007); Lintott, *Cicero*; Tatum (forthcoming commentary).

The translation reproduces that of *A Short Guide to Electioneering* (LACTOR 3, first edition) but with the addition of section headings which do not form part of the Latin text, and with the following changes:

[9]   'a Roman *eques* who belonged to no party' → 'a Roman *eques* who played no active part in politics'
[24] 'district and town' → 'district and town (*municipium*)'
[30] 'town, settlement or province' → 'town (*municipium*), settlement (*colonia*) or administrative area'
[31] 'provincial towns' → 'provincial towns (*municipia*)'
[53] 'have been in sympathy with them in your speeches' → 'have been a *popularis* in your speeches'

[1] **Introduction**

You possess all the gifts that men can acquire through natural ability, experience and diligence. However, because of our affection for one another I have not thought it out of place to send you the ideas which I have had as I pondered night and day over your candidacy. I do this, not that you may learn something new, but in order to gather together in one place, and in a logical arrangement, facts which seemed in themselves to be isolated and ill-defined.[1] Although natural talent is most important, it seems that it can be defeated by fraud in a matter that lasts only for a few months.[2]

[2] Consider what city this is, what you are seeking, who you are. Almost every day as you go down into the Forum, you must bear this in mind: 'I am a *novus homo*. I am seeking the consulship. This is Rome.'

Reputation for oratory

The fact that you are a *novus homo* will be made considerably less harsh by the reputation of your oratory; for oratory has always conferred great distinction. A man who is thought worthy to be the advocate of men of consular rank cannot be considered unworthy of the consulship.[3] Since you have this reputation to start with, and your position, whatever it is, is the result of this, come prepared to speak as though in each individual case a verdict were to be made on your whole character and ability.

[3] **Cicero's supporters**

See that the aids to this ability which I know are your special gifts are ready and available: remind yourself time and again of what Demetrius wrote about the study and practice of Demosthenes.[4] Secondly, see that people know how many friends you have and what sort of men they are. For what *novi homines* have possessed the advantages which you have? You have all the *publicani*, virtually all the *equites*, many *municipia* loyal to you alone, many men of every class whom you have defended, several *collegia*, and in addition very many young men who have been won over to you by the study of oratory, and a large and constant circle of *amici* in daily attendance.[5]

[4] **Maintain 'natural' supporters: cultivate *nobiles***

Take care to hold on to these advantages by giving them advice, by seeking their help and by using all possible means to ensure that those who are indebted to you realise that they will have no other chance to pay their debt; while those who wish to do you a service will have no other occasion to place you in their debt. One further thing which seems to help a *novus homo* is the goodwill of the *nobiles*, and particularly men of

---

[1] The admission that Cicero will not learn anything is, at first sight, strange. Cicero's *Letter to his brother Quintus*, 1.1 = SB Q1 is a long letter, giving advice on governing a province, written at a time (60/59) BC when Cicero had not done so, but Quintus had, for the last two years. He still writes, "I write not to tell you what to do ..."

[2] On bribery, see section 55 with footnotes.

[3] Cicero is not actually known to have defended any ex-consuls before being consul himself. His first known senatorial client was Fonteius in 69 BC, successfully defended against a charge of extortion.

[4] Demetrius of Phaleron (near Athens), born *c.*350 BC. Writer of various works, including literary criticism. Demosthenes (384–322 BC), the greatest Athenian orator. "Demetrius of Phaleron writes that when Demosthenes was not able to say the letter 'R' he practised until he could say it very clearly." (Cicero, *On Divination* 2.96).

[5] *Publicani* were businessmen who carried out public contracts auctioned by censors. They were the richest *equites*, and Cicero calls them "the flower of the equestrian order". For other terms, *novi homines, equites, municipia, collegia, amici* see glossary, pages 5–7.

consular rank. It is of advantage that the men into whose rank and number you wish to enter should themselves consider you to be worthy of entry.[6]

[5] Stress 'optimate', downplay 'popularis' credentials

These men you must cultivate diligently.[7] You must call upon them, persuade them that politically we have always been in sympathy with the *optimates* and have never in the least been supporters of the *populares*.[8] If we seem to have said anything characteristic of a *popularis* we did so with the intention of winning over Pompey[9] to our side, so that in our campaign for office we might have the man with the greatest influence either as an *amicus* or, at any rate, not as an opponent.[10]

[6] Cultivate young *nobiles*

Furthermore, take all pains to see that you have on your side young men of noble birth, and that you keep those whom you already have eager for your cause. They will bring great influence. You have very many of them; make sure that they know how much importance you attach to them.[11] If you have prevailed upon those who are not openly hostile to show active support for you, they will be of considerable benefit to you.

[7] Negligible threat from Galba and Cassius Longinus

There is another factor which makes up for your being a *novus homo*: the *nobiles* who are competing with you are of such a kind that no one would dare to say that they should profit more from their noble birth than you should from your merits. For who could look on Publius Galba and Lucius Cassius – men of noble birth – as candidates?[12] You can see that there are men from the noblest families who are not equal to you, because they are without vigour and ability.

[8] Antonius

But, you will argue, Antonius and Catiline are dangerous opponents.[13] Certainly they are! but a man who is vigorous, hard-working, without taint of crime, eloquent, and has influence among the men who decide events, should long for such men as competitors. For they have both been murderers since childhood, both are wanton and both are impecunious.

---

[6]   No doubt easier said than done! "Although plebeians reached other magistracies, the *nobiles* used to pass the consulship from one of their number to another. No *novus homo*, however distinguished he or his achievements might be, was considered worthy of that office, which it was thought he would pollute, as if unclean." (Sallust, *Jugurthine War* 63, written *c*. 41–40 BC about Marius' (successful) campaign of 107).

[7]   Cicero had already taken this advice – see his letters to Atticus, above.

[8]   For these terms, see glossary, pages 6.

[9]   See Pompey in Index of Names.

[10] Cicero had certainly taken a *popularis* position in 66 BC, as praetor, in his speech to the people, *On the Command of Gnaeus Pompeius*, advocating giving Pompey special command of the war against Mithridates, King of Pontus (Northern Turkey). But note his fears in his *Letter to Atticus* 1.1.2 (page 9) that he did not have Pompey's support. Then again, in his first speech as consul, he pledged to be a *popularis* – *Lege Agraria* 2.6, while giving his own definition as to what this meant.

[11] One such was Lucius Domitius Ahenobarbus, described by Cicero as 'the one man on whom my candidature particularly depends' (*Letter to Atticus*, 1.1.4 – see above, page 10).

[12] Publius Sulpicius Galba, see above, note on *Letter to Atticus* 1.1.1, page 9. Lucius Cassius Longinus had not been mentioned in Cicero's letter to Atticus as a likely or even possible rival, though Asconius, *preface*, shows that he did stand.

[13] Gaius Antonius: Cicero's fellow-praetor in 66 BC, and eventually, co-consul. Lucius Sergius Catilina: Cicero's arch-enemy in the consulship elections, and, of course, as the instigator of the Catilinarian conspiracy.

We have witnessed the confiscation of the property of Antonius; then we have heard him declare on oath that he could not contend at law in Rome on level terms with a Greek; we know that he was expelled from the Senate in a most scrupulous and honest scrutiny by the *censores*.[14] We have competed with him in the elections for the position of *praetor*, when he had Sabidius and Panthera[15] as *amici* since he did not have anyone whom he could put forward at the scrutiny of votes – and yet during his term of office he bought a mistress at the sales with the intention of keeping her openly in his house. In his campaign for the consulship he preferred to rob all the innkeepers in the course of a scandalous tour as *legatus*[16] rather than stay here and plead for the support of the people of Rome.

[9] Catiline

Now for your other competitor – heavens above, what's his claim to fame? Well, in the first place he possesses the same noble birth as Antonius. It's certainly not greater, is it?[17] No – but at least he is more courageous. In what respect? While Antonius is afraid of his own shadow, Catiline has no fear, even of the laws. For he was born amid his father's poverty, brought up amid the vices of his sister, blooded in the slaughter of citizens and initiated into public life with the murder of Roman *equites*.[18] For Sulla[19] had put Catiline in sole charge of those Gauls – we have not forgotten them – who at that time were mowing down the Titinii, the Nannii and the Tanusii;[20] among them Catiline murdered with his own hands a most honest man, Quintus Caecilius.[21] Caecilius was the husband of his sister; he was a Roman *eques* who played no active part in politics, a man ever peaceable by nature and at that time particularly so owing to his age.

[10] Catiline's killing of Gratidianus and other crimes

Need I now mention that you are competing for the consulship with a man who has beaten with cudgels Marcus Marius,[22] who was very popular with the Roman people – driving him all through the city while the people of Rome gazed on; who led him to a pyre and tortured him there with every form of cruelty; who, while Marius was still alive and breathing, beheaded him with his right hand, grasping the hair from the

---

[14] These three charges are all in Asconius [2]. The censors were senior magistrates, usually ex-consuls, elected every five years. Amongst their duties was to uphold the requirement of senators to be of good character. They could expel senators. Lintott, *Constitution* pages 71–2.

[15] These two are as obscure as Q. Cicero's comment implies.

[16] Here refers to a *libera legatio*, properly travel abroad to fulfil a religious vow, frequently abused to do private business at state expense. Cicero tried to legislate against the practice in his year as consul. See Lintott, *Constitution*, page 74.

[17] Catiline's family was 'patrician' – from the oldest nobility of Rome. Asconius [preface] places the patrician candidates in a separate category from the *nobiles*.

[18] For Sallust's hardly less extreme assessment, see Sallust, *Catiline*, 5.1–2.

[19] Sulla (Lucius Cornelius Sulla Felix) 138–78 BC. Twice led his armies against Rome. Plundered cities of the Greek East. Dealt severely with towns and areas of Italy opposed to Rome. Made himself dictator in 82/1 BC, and instituted proscriptions (legalised murder of personal and political opponents, and confiscation of their property: lists of the names of the proscribed were published in Rome and their killers were rewarded). Confiscated land was given to his veterans. As dictator Sulla also carried out much-needed reforms of the Senate. Having done this he resigned the dictatorship and soon retired to private life, dying shortly afterwards.

[20] Most likely, Quintus means individuals by the names of Titinius, Nanneius and Tanusius, not otherwise prominent.

[21] Asconius [2] mentions Tanusius and Caecilius, whose name should probably be Caucilius (Shackleton Bailey note to Loeb edition).

[22] Marcus Marius Gratidianus, whose murder is related, with differing details, by a wide range of sources (Plutarch, *Life of Sulla* 32; Sallust, *Histories* 1.44; Livy *Summary* 88; Valerius Maximus, 9.2.1; Lucan 2.160–73; Florus 2.9.26 and Asconius [2, 9, 18–19]). Gratidianus came from the same home town as Cicero (Arpinum) and was first cousin of Cicero's father.

top of his head with his left; who then carried the head on his hand while streams of blood poured between his fingers; who afterwards lived in the company of actors and gladiators so that he had the former to minister to his passion and the latter to abet his criminal schemes; who approached no shrine without leaving some disgraceful trace of his wickedness, even if he did not involve others in blame;[23] who made close friends with men like Curius and Annius in the Senate,[24] men like Sapala and Carvilius in the auction rooms and men like Pompilius and Vettius among the *equites*;[25] who shows such brazen wickedness, in a word such skill and success in his lust that he has violated young boys almost in the lap of their parents? Should I mention to you Africa, and the statements of witnesses?[26] You know them; see that you read them over more frequently. And yet I do not think that I ought to omit saying firstly that he left the court as poor as some of his judges had been before the trial; secondly that so odious is he that not a day passes without a fresh trial being demanded for him. His conduct is such that men are more afraid of him when he remains inactive than they are contemptuous of him if he does stir to action.

[11] **Example of Coelius, recent *novus homo***
How much better a chance of election you have been offered than another recent *novus homo*, Gaius Coelius. He had as competitors two men of the noblest birth whose other assets were of greater value even than their birth: they possessed outstanding ability, absolute integrity, had many fine achievements to their name, and showed consummate care and diligence in their election campaign. And yet Coelius, though much inferior in birth, and superior in almost no respect, defeated one of them.[27]

[12] **Two daggers against the state**
Thus if you make use of the assets bestowed on you by nature and by the studies which you have always pursued, if you do what the circumstances of the occasion demand – as you can and should do – the contest with these competitors, who are more remarkable for their crimes than distinguished by birth, will not be difficult. Can you find a single citizen so despicable that he wants to unsheathe two daggers upon the state in one election?[28]

[13] **The importance of the campaign**
Since I have explained what means you have and could have of overcoming the fact that you are a *novus homo*, I think I should now speak about the importance of the election campaign. You are a candidate for the consulship. No one believes you to be unworthy of this office, but many are envious. For you, an *eques*, are seeking the highest position in the state, highest in the sense that the same office confers much more distinction on a man who is brave, eloquent and free from crime than on others.

---

23   A reference to Catiline's alleged seduction of the Vestal Virgin, Fabia, sister of Cicero's wife – see Asconius [22].
24   Curius is also mentioned in Asconius [28] as a notorious gambler. Sallust names Curius and Quintus Annius as senatorial co-conspirators of Catiline (Sallust, *Catiline* 17.3).
25   Sapala and Carvilius, Pompilius and Vettius are not otherwise known.
26   See Asconius [8].
27   Gaius Coelius Caldus was consul in 94 BC, alongside Lucius Domitius Ahenobarbus, presumably father of the man of the same name who helped Cicero (*Letter to Atticus* 1.1.4, page 10). It is not known whom he beat. Cicero, *pro Murena* 17 names the previous three *novi homines* to be consuls before him as Gaius Marius (107 and for a seventh time in 86), Titus Didius (98) and Coelius (94). He omits Gaius Norbanus, consul in 83.
28   The same metaphor is used by Cicero in his *Speech as a Candidate* – Asconius [27].

Do not imagine that those who have held this office fail to see what standing you will have once you have obtained it. I have a suspicion that those who belong to consular families but have not yet gained the position of their forefathers are envious of you, apart from any who are your very close friends.[29] *Novi homines* who have held the office of *praetor*, I presume, except for those who are obliged to you for some service, are reluctant to be outstripped by you in office.

[14] Sources of opposition

Indeed, I know full well that you are aware how many among the people are jealous of you, how many have become hostile to a *novus homo*, because of the pattern of events in the past few years.[30] Some of them must even be angry with you as a result of those cases you have pleaded. Furthermore, look around you and consider whether, because you applied yourself with such zeal to increasing the glory of Pompey, those whom you consider to be your *amici* for this reason, really are on your side.[31]

[15] Work hard

Therefore, since you are seeking the highest office of state, and you see the interests that are lined up against you, you should consider every detail and apply attention, diligence and hard work to everything.

[16] *Amici*

A campaign for election to magistracy can be divided into two kinds of activity: firstly to gain the support of one's *amici*, secondly to win the goodwill of the people.

The support of one's *amici* should be secured by kindnesses done and repaid, by long-standing acquaintance and by a charming and affable nature. But the word "*amicus*" has a wider application in an election campaign than in the rest of life. Anyone who shows any sympathy towards you, who pays attention to you, who frequents your house, should be reckoned among your "*amici*". On the other hand, it is most important to be kind and warm-hearted to those who really are your *amici* through relationship of marriage or blood, through a *collegium* or some other connection.

[17] Your household

Next you must take great trouble to see that anyone who is closely connected with you, and particularly members of your household, supports you eagerly and wants you to be as successful as possible; then too those of your tribe, neighbours, *clientes*,[32] *liberti* too and last of all even your slaves. For in general every rumour which becomes the common gossip of the forum originates from sources within one's own home.

[18] Men of influence

It is necessary to have *amici* of every kind: for the sake of appearance, make friends with men who are distinguished in rank and title (these, though they may not actively

---

[29] See footnote 6 above.

[30] Quintus Cicero may have in mind Marius' dubious reputation or that of Norbanus whom Cicero himself omits (see footnote 27).

[31] See section [5] and footnote 10.

[32] *Clientes* were men who bound themselves to the service (especially support in the assemblies) of men of superior birth, wealth or power: in return the patron (*patronus*) would guarantee protection, especially defence in the lawcourts. See Lintott, *Constitution* 178–181.

support the campaign, nonetheless confer some prestige upon the candidate); in order to make good the justice of your claim, make friends with the magistrates – in particular the consuls, and secondly the *tribuni plebis*;[33] in order to get the votes of the *centuriae*, make friends with men who have exceptional influence. Make special efforts to win over and keep loyal to yourself such men as (because of your influence) have or hope to have the votes of a tribe or a *centuria*,[34] or who can help you in some other way. For in recent years, men of ambition have worked hard with zeal and effort to be able to obtain what they wanted from the members of their tribe. You should endeavour by whatever means you can to see that these men show their support for you with a genuine sincerity.

[19] Support from *collegia* of men represented by Cicero in court

But if men were sufficiently grateful, all these sources of influence ought to be available to you, as I am confident that they in fact are. For within the last two years you have laid under obligation to yourself four *collegia*,[35] those of Gaius Fundanus, Quintus Gallus, Gaius Cornelius and Gaius Orchivus – all men of the greatest influence for a campaign.[36] In entrusting their cases to your care I know what the members of their *collegia* have taken on themselves and promised you: I was there. Thus you must see that at this time you demand from these men their debts, by frequent advice, seeking their votes, and by careful encouragement, so that they realise they will never have another opportunity of showing their gratitude. Certainly, they will be encouraged to show active support for you in the expectation of your future returns to them and by your recent benefits to them.

[20] Call in debts of gratitude

Now since your election campaign is founded to a very large degree upon the sort of *amici* you have won as a result of your defences in the courts, see that every single person whom you hold bound to you by some tie has his personal role well-defined and specified. As you have never been a nuisance to any of them in anything, see that they understand that you have saved up for this moment all the debts which you think they owe you.

[21] Support in return for past legal representation

For there are three things which act as particular incentives for men to be well-disposed and give their support to a campaign: a favour, hope, and spontaneous goodwill. You must pay attention to ways of making sure of each of these.

---

33 For the *tribuni plebis* or tribunes of the people, see glossary, page 7.

34 Every Roman citizen was officially a member of one of 35 tribes. The local origin of these had been diluted by the registration of newly enfranchised Italian communities in tribes, but a range of evidence suggests considerable importance of tribes (see Lintott, *Constitution* 50–5 and 176–7). A letter of Cicero to Atticus of June 60 (2.1.9 = SB A21) talks of a candidate for tribune, Favonius, winning Cicero's tribe (presumably with Cicero's active support) more decisively than his own, but losing that of a Lucceius who presumably had tried to deliver the votes of his tribe. There existed *divisores* responsible for distributing benefits from patrons to members of a tribe: their name becomes a byword for electoral bribery (*OLD* 2b). Horace satirises the would-be politician having to put up with being introduced to 'this man who has a lot of influence in the Fabian tribe, this one in the Veline; another who gives and takes the *fasces* and seats of office from whomsoever he pleases.' – Horace, *Epistles* 1.6.52–54 (*c*. 21–20 BC).

35 'organizations even more obscure than the tribes' Lintott, *Constitution* page 177.

36 66–65 BC – defence of Gaius Fundanius (unknown charge), known from *SGE* and some later quotations. In 65 BC – defence of Gaius Cornelius on a treason charge – see footnote 52. In 65 BC – defence of Gaius Orchivus, praetor alongside Cicero in 66 BC (*pro Cluentio* 94, 147) on unknown charge. In 64 BC – defence of Quintus Gallius on charge of election bribery, also known from Asconius [12] and later quotations. For chronology of these trials, see Appendix of J. Powell & J. Paterson, eds, *Cicero the Advocate*.

You can win men over to thinking that they have sufficient reason to support your cause by the smallest of favours, so those whom you have actually saved (and there are very many of them) cannot fail to understand that if they do not do enough for you at this vital time they will never be respected by anyone. However, there still remains a need to canvass them in person, and get them to think that we appear to be indebted in our turn to those who have so far been our debtors.

[22] Support in return for future hopes

As for those who are bound to us by hopes – a class still more zealous and eager on our behalf – you must give the impression that your assistance is always ready and at their disposal, and also make them perceive that you take great notice of their services, so that you seem to observe and appreciate fully whatever each one bestows on you.

[23] Support from spontaneous goodwill

The third class of supporters are those with spontaneous goodwill. This you will have to strengthen by showing gratitude, by adapting what you say to the particular circumstances which seem to make a man favourably disposed towards you, by demonstrating equal goodwill to them, and by encouraging them to hope for a closer *amicitia*. In your dealings with each of these three kinds of supporter, you must weigh up and judge for yourself the value of every one of them to you, so that you can decide how much attention should be paid to them by you, and what you can expect and demand from them.

[24] Men with influence in their own *municipia*

There are some men who exercise influence in their own district and town (*municipium*),[37] – prosperous and industrious people who, despite their having shown no previous interest in your cause, may well work their hardest for a candidate when the time comes – if there is one to whom they feel indebted, or whom they wish to help. You must pay attention to such men, so that they will come to realise that you know what you can depend on from them, that you take notice of what you actually receive from them, and that you remember what you have already gained. But there are others who can achieve nothing, or who are even unpopular in their tribe, and have not the ability or mind to make efforts on the spur of the moment. See that you distinguish these, in order not to put greater dependence on any of them than will be justified by the small amount of help they provide.

[25] *Amicitia* in election campaigns I

Although you ought to be able to rely on and be provided with *amicitiae* that have been gained and confirmed already, yet even during the campaign a great number can be gained which are very useful. For, despite the various inconveniences, to stand in an election has this advantage at least: it is perfectly respectable to do things which would be impossible in ordinary life. You can attach to yourself in *amicitia* those whom at any other time you could not allow to be associated with you in such a way without your appearing absurd; but in an election, unless you act in this way (quite deliberately, and with many people), you will give the impression of being no kind of candidate.

---

[37] Town (Latin *municipium*): a number of Italian towns had been self-governing even before their inhabitants received Roman citizenship in the 80s; Cicero came from one (Arpinum) and they were centres of support for him. *See CAH* ix², pages 127–8.

[26] *Amicitia* in election campaigns II

Now I say this to you quite confidently, that there is no one (unless he is closely connected in some way with one of your rivals) whom you could not easily get to strive by some act of service to win your *amicitia* and indebtedness, if only you set your mind to it. All that is needed is that he should realise that you value his company highly, that you are acting in earnest, that he is placing himself in a good position, and that the *amicitia* will not be a fleeting one, disappearing with the conclusion of the election campaign, but will be solid and lasting.

[27] *Amicitia* in election campaigns III

Believe me, no one of any sense will let this opportunity of gaining your *amicitia* slip by – especially since your fellow-candidates happen to be the sort of men whose *amicitia* ought to be despised and avoided, and who could not even begin to put into practice the advice which I am giving you, let alone carry it out properly.

[28] Antonius' lack of personal contacts

How, for example, could Antonius start to attach men to himself, and invite them to become his *amici*, when he is incapable by himself even of calling them by their names?[38] There seems to be nothing more foolish than to imagine that a man whom you do not know is devoted to you. It would take an incredible reputation and tremendous prestige, allied to stupendous achievements, for a man to be elected to office by men who did not know him without canvassers. So for a man who is an idle scoundrel, who is without any readiness to do a good turn, or any real ability, a man with a bad reputation and no *amici* – for such a man to take precedence over someone backed by a great crowd, and armed with the good opinion of all, is something which could not happen without the grossest of negligence.

[29] Use all contacts

For this reason, you must take care to secure your strength in each *centuria* with a number of different *amicitiae*. Above all – and this is obvious – make connections among the senators and *equites* of Rome, and then with industrious and important men of other ranks. Many who live in the city are active; many *liberti* have influence in the forum and use it keenly.[39] Wherever possible (either through your own devices or mutual *amici*) work with utmost care to make these eager for your cause: visit them in person, send your agents, and show that you are full of kindness for them.

[30] And all areas

After this, you must concern yourself with the whole city, all the *collegia*, districts and neighbourhoods. If you unite the leading men in these to yourself in *amicitia*, you will find it easy to get the crowds following in their wake. Next you must have in your thoughts and memory a list in which each town in Italy is entered according to the tribe to which it belongs,[40] in such a way that there is no single town (*municipium*),

---

38 On the importance of names, see footnote 49.
39 *Liberti* – freed slaves. Some freedmen became prosperous and influential by acting as business agents for senators, whose trading activities were restricted by law. See S. Treggiari, *Roman Freedmen in the Late Republic*.
40 On tribes, see footnote 34 above.

settlement (*colonia*) or administrative area[41] – in fact, no place at all in Italy – in which you have not gained a sufficiently firm foothold.

[31] **Including outside Rome**
Search out and discover men in every area; get to know them, visit them, strengthen their loyalty, make sure that in their own vicinity they are campaigning for you, and pleading your cause as though they themselves were the candidate. They will seek your *amicitia* if they see that you desire theirs. Adopt the kind of speech which will be effective in bringing them to realise this. Men from the countryside and from provincial towns (*municipia*) think that they are our *amici* if we know their names; but if they think they are gaining some protection for themselves they will not lose the chance of offering their assistance. Other people (your rivals in particular) ignore such men completely; but you both recognise them and will easily be able to get to know them; if you do not, there can be no *amicitia*.

[32] **Influence in tribes, *municipia, collegia***
But this, though important, is not enough: the best thing is the hope of gaining assistance and *amicitia*, so that you may not seem merely to be able to call them by their name, but actually to be a close *amicus*. So when you have those men who can exert great influence among their fellow-tribesmen working hard on your behalf in the *centuriae*, because of their private ambition, and have got others too who have power in a particular section of the tribes (because of their connections in their *municipium* or neighbourhood, or through membership of a *collegium*) firmly established on your side – then you should feel extremely optimistic.[42]

[33] **The *centuriae equitum***
Now it seems to me that the *centuriae equitum* can be secured much more easily by constant attention.[43] Firstly identify the *equites*; there are not many of them. Then visit them; they are very young, so that you can get them to become your *amici* much more easily. Now you will have with you all the best and most zealous young men. Also, since you yourself have the status of *eques*, they will follow the authority of this rank, if only you exhibit care to strengthen your support in these *centuriae* by individual *amicitiae* as well as by the general goodwill of the *equites*. It is excellent and honourable to have the enthusiasm of the young in your canvassing, in meeting people, announcing your programme and accompanying you personally.

[34] **Those in attendance**
And since I have touched on the question of those who will be in attendance to you, this is something else which must be treated with great care, so that you see to it that you have a daily following of all kinds, classes and ages of people.[44] For from that

---

[41] The term *praefectura*, previously translated as 'province' refers to a town in Italy, for example Capua (Velleius 2.44.4) in which justice was administered under supervision of a *praefectus* sent from Rome.

[42] On tribes, see footnote 34 above.

[43] The 18 centuries with the highest property-qualification, the *centuriae equitum*, voted first, and it was common for the other *centuriae* to follow their lead.

[44] In this section and those following, Q. Cicero does not use the terms *cliens* or *patronus*, but *amici* [39] and it is not clear whether the traditional picture of *clientela* being at the heart of political life is correct. 'What can be asserted categorically, however, is that a rigorous examination by P.A. Brunt of the evidence for the operations of *clientela* has shown that the evidence available to us contains no valid support for the notion that the key to Roman politics lies here.' F.G.B. Millar, *The Crowd in Rome in the Late Republic*, page 9, referring to Brunt, *The Fall of the Roman Republic*, chapter 8, "*Clientela*".

range of support it would be possible to hazard a guess what the numerical strength and quality of your backing will be when it comes to the actual election. Now there are three groups within this category: those who pay their respects when they visit you at home, those who are led down with you to the Forum, and finally those who accompany you wherever you go.[45]

[35] Those visiting

For those who greet you – who are less select as a group, and, as the custom is today, visit more than one candidate – it is necessary to make it clear that even this minimal duty which they perform is pleasing you. For those who visit your home,[46] let them see that you are aware of it: either tell their *amici*, who will report back to them, or on occasion tell them to their face. Sometimes men who visit several candidates and see that there is one who particularly notices their attentions will devote themselves to that one and abandon the rest, so that gradually they become firm supporters rather than neutrals, and ardent canvassers instead of waverers. But keep this principle firmly in mind: if you hear that one who has promised himself to you is "suspect", as they say (or if you yourself have perceived that this is so), pretend not to have heard it or to know it; should anyone wish to justify himself to you, believing that he has fallen into suspicion, declare that you have never doubted his good intentions, nor ought to doubt them. For he who does not think he is proving satisfactory as an *amicus* cannot possibly be so. But you must know each person's mind, so that you can decide how much confidence you can place on anyone.

[36] Those accompanying you to the Forum

Acknowledge and demonstrate that the duty performed by those who escort you down to the Forum is more pleasing to you to the extent that it is greater than that of those who visit you at home. As far as possible, descend to the Forum at fixed times: a large daily gathering escorting you to the Forum is a source of great esteem and honour.[47]

[37] Regular followers

The third category is that persistent band of followers. Among these, take care that those who come of their own free will realise that you are eternally grateful to them for their services; as to those who are in your debt, exact from them this plain duty: those whose business commitments and age allow it should attend you in person; those who cannot themselves accompany you must appoint someone connected with them for this service. To this I urge you emphatically; I believe it is most important for you always to be surrounded by people.

[38] Those previously represented in court by Cicero

Another thing which brings great praise and high prestige is for those who have been defended by you, and saved and acquitted by the lawcourts because of you, to be with

---

[45] Cicero, *pro Murena* 70–71 imagines his opponents complaining that those who accompanied Murena had been bribed and indignantly defends the right of humble citizens to earn or return favours by electoral attendance.

[46] Cicero's famous house on the Palatine was not bought until December 62 BC, for the vast sum of 3.5 million sesterces – see *Letter to Friends* 5.6.2 = SB F4.

[47] Cicero boasts of crowds accompanying him home at the end of his consulship and when appearing as witness against Clodius in 61 BC – *Letters to Atticus* 1.16.5 = SB A16. Cicero himself mentions accompanying a consular candidate in *Letters to Atticus* 2.1.5 = SB A21.

you. You can demand this from them in no uncertain way, since at no expense some have kept their property through your help, some their good name, some safety and their whole livelihood; there will be no future opportunity for repaying to you their gratitude, so you may insist that they reward you by this service to you.

[39] Don't trust people too easily

Now since I have been talking all this time about the attentions of *amici*, I should not overlook under this heading one area which demands special caution. Everything is full of deceit, traps and treachery. This is not the right time for a long diatribe on the subject – about ways to distinguish the person who is sincere from the fraud – all that can be done at the moment is to give some advice. Your high qualities will force the men to feign *amicitia* for you and at the same time to be jealous. So remember that saying of Epicharmus: "The essence of wisdom is this: don't trust people too easily."[48]

[40] Three kinds of opponents

And when you have established the support of your *amici*, you must also give thought to the methods and variety of opposition and attack. There are three kinds of adversary: the first are those whom you have harmed; the second are those who dislike you, but without reason; and the third are those who are close *amici* of your rivals. As for those injured by you, since you have spoken against them on behalf of an *amicus*, be highly apologetic to them, recall the exigencies of the situation, and foster the hope that they will receive your involvement in their affairs with equal zeal and earnestness if they become your *amici*. Those who have no reason for their dislike of you, you must strive to win over from this unfortunate state of mind by some kindness, or offer of hope, or by showing your concern on their behalf. With those who are alienated from you because of *amicitia* with your competitors, use the same tactics as with the other groups; if you can convince them, show that you are well-disposed even to your rivals.

[41] Standing among the people

I have said enough on the subject of fostering *amicitiae*; now I must speak briefly about the other part of the campaign – that which is concerned with your standing among the people. This requires that you show knowledge of people's names,[49] that you have winning manners, persistence, generosity, reputation and confidence in your public programme.

[42] Recognition of men

Firstly, concerning your recognition of men: see that you show this quite clearly, and strive to improve every day. To me nothing seems better designed to secure popular favour. Next, make up your mind that what your nature lacks must seem to come to you naturally. For although you are not without that courtesy which befits a good and well-bred man, you badly need flattery, which, though disgraceful in the rest of one's

---

[48] Epicharmus: writer of Greek comedy, active in Sicily in the first quarter of the fifth century BC. Quintus oddly writes his name in Greek letters, but uses a Latin version of the quotation. The Greek original is quoted by Marcus Cicero in a letter to Atticus of 15 March 60 BC (1.19.8 = SB A19).

[49] *Nomenclatio*: wealthy Romans might have a special slave called a *nomenclator*. In Cicero's speech *pro Murena* 77, he attacks the prosecutor, Cato, the 'whiter than white' Stoic philosopher and politician for having such a *nomenclator*. Plutarch (whose source may be that passage of *pro Murena*) reports that Cicero took remembering names very seriously (Plutarch, *Life of Cicero* 7), though at least on his return from exile in September 57, he used a *nomenclator* (*Letter to Atticus* 4.1.4 = SB A73).

life, is essential while electioneering.[50] It is certainly a bad thing when it causes a man's deterioration by constantly agreeing with him; but when it makes him more amenable, it is not so much to be deplored, but rather is indispensable for a true candidate, whose expression, countenance and language are to be adapted and accommodated to the particular wishes and moods of whomever he meets.

[43] Persistence

No instruction is needed about persistence – the very word reveals its nature. It is extremely important not to go off anywhere; but the real reward of persistence comes not just from being present in Rome and the Forum, but from incessant canvassing, frequently revisiting the same people, and (as far as possible) not allowing anyone to be able to say that he was not canvassed (and well and earnestly canvassed) by you.[51]

[44] Good manners

Good manners cover a wide range of activities. They exist in one's private life, and although this does not affect the common people directly, the approval of one's *amici* in this respect can please them. They are to be found also at banquets, so make sure that these are celebrated – both by yourself and your *amici* – on many occasions and in each tribe.[52] It operates too in services which you do, which should be made public and available; see that there is access to you at day and night: let not only your house's doors be open, but your face and expression, which are the doors to your soul. If you betray feelings of reserve and concealment by the look on your face, there is little point in having your doors open. Men do not simply look for promises for themselves, though this is what they want first of all from a candidate, but they want the attachment to be expansive and bounteous.

[45] Dealing with requests

From this it naturally follows that you should show that whatever you intend to do, you intend to do willingly and with enthusiasm. What is more difficult, and a requirement of this particular occasion rather than something that comes naturally to you, is to refuse in a pleasant manner what you cannot do, or even not to refuse; the former course is that taken by a good man, the latter is that of a good candidate for election. For when a request is made for something which you could not undertake without dishonour or harm to your cause (as if someone asks us to take up some case against one of our friends), the refusal ought to be that of a gentleman, tactfully showing the impossibility of the demand, letting him see that you are grieved that you must turn it down, and convincing him that you will make up for this on another occasion.[53]

---

[50] Cicero's *De oratore*, written in 55 BC, aims to show what an orator should be and do. Cicero represents his main model, Lucius Licinius Crassus (consul 95 BC), as describing his canvassing at elections as involving 'demeaning myself, that is seeking votes by flattery – something which cannot be done well except by demeaning oneself.' (*De oratore* 1.112).

[51] For the dangers of boring the electorate, however, see *pro Murena* 21 (below, page 41).

[52] As consul, Cicero got the Senate to ratify a decree specifying that a law on electoral bribery passed by the consuls of 67 BC should be taken as prohibiting, amongst other things, the indiscriminate giving of dinners (*pro Murena* 67). Yet later in the same speech he suggests that the parsimonious contribution of Quintus Aelius Tubero to a public funeral banquet in 129 BC cost him the praetorship (*pro Murena* 75–6).

[53] An example of such a situation can be found in Cicero, *Letter to Atticus* 1.1.4 (see page 10), where Cicero refused to represent Atticus' uncle against an *amicus* (and client of a vital aristocratic supporter).

[46] **Words more attractive than deeds**

I have heard a man say of certain advocates to whom he had offered his case: "The words of the man who refused my case pleased me more than those of the man who took it up." This is an illustration of how men are attracted by words and appearances more than the fact of a kindness. The former of the two courses I mentioned is to be commended to you; the latter will be rather more difficult to commend to you, a disciple of Plato;[54] yet I will say what your circumstances require. For those men whom you say you will not help because of some obligation or necessity can nevertheless leave you without a grudge and in an even temper; but those whom you refused to help because you claim to be prevented by the business of your *amici* or by cases that are more important, or that you have already begun, leave you with feelings of hostility. All men naturally prefer you to lie to them than to refuse them your aid.

[47] **Make promises (1)**

Gaius Cotta, a master at campaigning, used to say that it was his custom to promise his services to all, so long as the request was not contrary to some obligation, but actually to bestow them only on those people on whom he thought them best placed; he refused no one, because often something happened which caused the man to whom he had promised his aid to be unable to make use of it, and himself to have fewer engagements than he had at first expected.[55] The house of a man who only took on as much as he saw he could accomplish could not possibly be filled with supporters. Things which you have not thought of may by chance take place, while that which you believe you have well in hand may not happen for some reason or another. The last thing to happen is for the man to whom you have told a lie to be angry.

[48] **Make promises (2)**

To make a promise is not definite; it allows postponement, and affects only a few people. A refusal alienates people immediately, and in greater numbers. For many more people make requests to be allowed to make use of another's services than actually use them. Thus it is better that some of these people are angry with you on occasion in the Forum, rather than that they should all be angry with you all the time in your home – particularly since they are much more angry with those who refuse them than at the man whom they see to be prevented from keeping his promise for reasons which show that he would be eager to carry it out if it were at all possible.

[49] **Winning over the people**

In case I seem to have digressed from my topic, by discussing these matters in a section of the campaign that deals with the people, I will show the connection: all these matters have to do with one's reputation among the people rather than with the support of one's *amici*. There is an element which concerns the latter, namely to give helpful advice, to be zealous in serving their interests, and to aid them when in danger. However, at this point I am speaking about the means by which you can win over the

---

54 Famous Athenian philosopher (429–347 BC), who stressed the importance of acting morally. In a letter to Atticus (4.16.3 = SB A89), Cicero refers to Plato as 'that god of ours'.

55 Gaius Aurelius Cotta, a distinguished orator (Cicero brackets him with Sulpicius as the best of his day – *Brutus* 182–3). He was consul in 75 BC and died in 73 BC.

populace in such a way that your house may be filled by night, that many people may be attached to your cause in the hope of your protection, that they may leave your house better disposed towards you than when they entered, and that as many people as possible may hear excellent reports about you.

[50] Reputation

It follows, then, that I must speak about reputation – and you must pay very careful attention. But what has been said throughout the earlier part of my discourse is equally important for the vigorous spreading of a good reputation – a name for public speaking, the enthusiastic support of the *equites* and the *publicani*;[56] the goodwill of the *nobiles*, a following of young men, the constant attendance of those who have been defended by you, and a large number of people from the *municipia* who can be seen to have come to support you. This will cause people to say and think that you know people well and address them as friends, that you seek their support persistently and with diligence, and that you are kind and generous. In this way your house may be full of supporters by night, with a crowd present from all classes, your speech may please all, your deeds and efforts many; you will achieve all that is possible by your toil, skill and diligence – not just so that men may give a report to the people, but that the people itself may be actively involved in your interests.

[51] Recent speeches gaining popular support

You have already gained the support of the city crowds, and of those who attend the gatherings of the people, by your lavish praise of Pompey, your undertaking of the case of Manilius and your defence of Cornelius.[57] We must now stir up that support which till now no one has had without the goodwill of distinguished men. Furthermore, people must be made to realise that the goodwill of Pompey towards you is immense and that for you to gain the office which you are seeking fits in perfectly with his plans.[58]

[52] Put up a good spectacle yourself and smear your enemies

Last of all, see that your whole campaign is full of show; that it is glorious and colourful, and pleasing to the people; that it has a fine appearance and dignity; furthermore, if it is by any means possible, see that your competitors are smeared with an evil reputation – which fits their characters – for crime, vice or bribery.[59]

---

[56]   For *publicani*, see footnote 5.

[57]   In 66 BC, as praetor, Cicero made a speech to the people, *On the Command of Gnaeus Pompeius*, advocating giving Pompey special command of the war against Mithridates, King of Pontus (Northern Turkey). Such a law hardly required Cicero's support or oratory to be passed. Rather Cicero hoped to gain political support from his stance (note his fears in his letter to Atticus (1.1) that he did not have Pompey's support). In 66/5 Cicero defended the tribune Manilius, proposer of the law on Pompey's special command, against an uncertain charge. Cicero defended Gaius Cornelius on a charge of treason in 65 BC. Cornelius, as tribune of the people in 67 BC had incurred the hostility of parts of the Senate for measures aimed at preventing loans to provincial envoys being made at ruinous rates of interest. The measure was popular, but the Senate had found another tribune to veto it and violence had ensued. Cornelius was charged with treason. This speech does not survive, but Asconius' commentary does, and includes detailed explanation of the circumstances (Asconius 57C – 62C). In all three of these recent and very high profile speeches, Cicero can be seen taking a popular line.

[58]   Clearly a huge exaggeration – see *Letters to Atticus* 1.1.2, 1.2.2 (pages 9 and 11).

[59]   Cicero certainly heeded this advice, see his *Speech as a Candidate against C. Antonius and L. Catilina.*

[53] Avoid policy

You must take very good care in your campaign that men have high hopes and a good impression of your programme: however in your canvassing, you should not adopt a definite policy – either in the meetings of the Senate or of the people. You should maintain the following position: that the Senate will reckon that, in accordance with your way of life up till now, you will be a defender of their prestige; that the Roman *equites* together with loyal and wealthy citizens, considering your career, think that you will be eager for peace and quiet; while the people think, in as far as you have been a *popularis* in your speeches (at least in their meetings and in the courts) you will not be hostile to their interests.

[54] The problems of Rome

These then are the ideas which have occurred to me in regard to the first two of the morning reflections which I suggested you should bear in mind as you go down daily to the Forum: "I am a *novus homo*. I am a candidate for the consulship." The third one remains: "This is Rome", a city made up of an admixture of peoples where much trickery, deceit and vice of every kind is to be found, where we will have to put up with the arrogance and insolence, the spite and pride, the hatred and interference of many men. It is obvious to me that a man who is working amid the deep-rooted and widespread evils of so many men needs great skill and tact to avoid stumbling, scandal and trickery, and to be the one man suited to so great a variety of character, opinion and feeling.

[55] Look out for opponents' bribery

Therefore keep to the path you have started on: excel in your public speaking. It is this which influences and attracts men in Rome, and deters them from standing in your way and harming you. Now in one particular aspect the state does have a fault: when bribery has intervened, people are apt to forget virtue and merit.[60] See that you fully realise your own power – that is that you are able to instil in your competitors a real fear of the courts and legal action; see that they know that you are watching and keeping an eye on them. They will be afraid not only of your attention and the power and influence of your public speaking, but particularly of the support of the *equites* for you.

[56] Without looking too intent on prosecutions

I do not want you to parade these activities to them so that it appears that you are already intent on accusations in court,[61] but so that you may more easily obtain your own objectives by causing them the fear that this might happen. Strive openly with all your strength and ability so that we may obtain what we are seeking. I am certain that no election is so stained with bribery that no *centuriae* return a candidate to whom they are bound by some strong tie, without bribes.

---

[60] Bribery (*ambitus*) was a significant issue in politics at this time. There was probably legislation *c*.81 BC, and certainly in 67, 63 and 52. Both consuls elected for 65 were convicted for *ambitus* (Asconius, *in Corneliam* 75C, Cicero, *pro Sulla* 50, Sallust, *Cat.* 18.2). Murena, elected for 62, was also prosecuted (Cicero, *pro Murena*). In 54 BC, all four candidates for the consulship were prosecuted – Cicero, *Letters to Atticus* 4.17.5 and 4.18.3 = SB 91, 92.

[61] Cicero criticises his opponent Sulpicius for exactly this in *pro Murena* 43 (below, page 45).

[57] **Reducing the importance of bribery**

Thus if we are alert – as is fitting considering the importance of our business; if we inspire our well-wishers; if we allot to those men of influence who are our followers each his own task; if we hold out fear of the courts before our competitors, create anxiety in their agents and restrain those who pay out the bribes by the same means – then we can see to it that there is no bribery and that it has no importance.

[58] **Conclusion**

These are the matters – it is not that I thought that I knew about them any better than you, but that in view of your commitments I could more easily collect them in one place and send them to you written out in detail. Now while they are not being put down with the intention of being relevant to all who are seeking office, but to you in particular and this election campaign of yours, I should like you to tell me if you think anything should be altered or completely removed, or if anything has been omitted. For I want this handbook on electioneering to be considered complete in every detail.

ASCONIUS' COMMENTARY ON CICERO'S SPEECH AS A CANDIDATE

Jerome's *World Chronicle* notes in AD 76 that the well-known historian Quintus Asconius Pedianus went blind aged 73 and died 12 years later. Asconius wrote commentaries on Cicero's speeches. Commentaries on five speeches survive, possibly in an abridged version. They were written between AD 54 and 57, ostensibly to help his sons still young enough (perhaps therefore in mid-twenties and not yet quaestors) to need guidance about procedures in the Senate. Asconius is a reliable scholar and one with first-hand experience of senatorial procedure, albeit under the principate, and access to written works, including by Cicero, which have not survived. His commentary on Cicero's speech as a candidate is invaluable both for his own historical comments and for preserving part of this speech which does not otherwise survive. Asconius provides background information on the election candidates and a very good flavour of the sorts of accusations Cicero made against his two main rivals. We need to remember that Cicero was addressing the Senate in this speech, but there is no reason to assume that he would have tempered his accusations in other election speeches. It is worth noting that although defamation (*iniuria*) was illegal, invective ('which sets out publicly to denigrate a named individual' – *Oxford Classical Dictionary*) was a recognised form of literature, with five different literary terms applied to different kinds of verbal abuse. Victims responded in kind, rather than by suing for damages. (See, for example, Syme, *Roman Revolution* pages 151–2.)

Numbering of Asconius' text is traditionally given by reference to page numbers in Clark's Oxford Classical Text of Asconius. These numbers appear in the margin. Asconius labelled his title, preface and epilogue as such: I have, in addition, numbered the main text according to passages quoted from Cicero's speech.

Asconius' principle in his commentary is to quote from Cicero and then to explain. Cicero's words, quoted by Asconius, appear **in bold**, Asconius' explanation in normal font. To avoid confusion, my notes appear as numbered footnotes.

SPEECH GIVEN IN THE SENATE AS A CANDIDATE AGAINST HIS ELECTION RIVALS, GAIUS ANTONIUS AND LUCIUS CATILINE.　　82C

This speech was delivered in the consulship of L. Caesar and C. Figulus [64 BC], the year after he had spoken for Cornelius.

Preface

Cicero had six rivals in his campaign for the consulship: two were patricians, P. Sulpicius Galba and L. Sergius Catiline; four were plebeians, two of whom were *nobiles*: C. Antonius, the son of the orator M. Antonius, and L. Cassius Longinus; the other two being merely not the first in their families to achieve office: Q. Cornificius, and C. Licinius Sacerdos.[62] Cicero alone of his rivals was of equestrian status by birth;

---

[62]　Asconius distinguishes between patricians (the oldest aristocracy), *nobiles* (descendants of a consul), and those with a senatorial, but not consular, ancestor. Since 342 BC the consuls could not both be patricians.

and he lost his father during the election campaign.[63] The rest of his rivals conducted themselves with restraint: Q. Cornificius and Galba were thought sound and virtuous men, Sacerdos was not known for any lack of principle; Cassius, though at that time he seemed more dull than vicious, was revealed a few months later to be in Catiline's conspiracy and to have been behind its most bloodthirsty proposals.[64] These four, therefore, were all but finished. Catiline and Antonius, however, though their lifestyle was absolutely notorious, were nonetheless very strong candidates. For the two of them had formed an election pact, with the very strong support of Marcus Crassus and Gaius Julius Caesar, aimed at preventing Cicero being elected consul. This is why this speech attacks only Catiline and Antonius. The occasion for Cicero making a speech of this sort in the Senate was that with blatant electoral malpractice increasing day by day because of the extraordinarily arrogant behaviour of Catiline and Antonius, the Senate had decreed that a law on electoral malpractice should be passed with further increased added penalties. The tribune of the people, Q. Mucius Orestinus, had vetoed this. At that point, with the Senate particularly angry at the veto, Cicero rose and launched his attack upon the election pact of Catiline and Antonius a few days before polling day.

83C

[1] **I maintain, members of the Senate, that last night Catiline and Antonius, together with their agents, met at the home of a certain *nobilis*, well-known and recognised in the business of giving large-scale funding.**
He refers to the home of either Julius Caesar or Marcus Crassus.[65] For they were the bitterest and most powerful of Cicero's opponents in seeking the consulship, because they were beginning to realise that his reputation amongst voters was increasing by the day. Cicero himself notes this in his *Political Memoirs*;[66] and he accuses Marcus Crassus of having been behind the conspiracy formed by Catiline and Piso in the consulship of Cotta and Torquatus [65 BC], the year before this speech was delivered.[67]

84C

[2] **For what *amicus* can he have when he has slaughtered so many citizens? What clients, when he has said that he could not, in his own homeland, compete in a fair trial against a foreigner?**[68]
It is said that Catiline had committed brutal crimes as a partisan of Sulla.[69] Cicero also goes on to name those killed – Quintus Caecilius, Marcus Volumnius, and Lucius

---

63   A rare demonstrable mistake from Asconius: Cicero's father died on 23 November 68 BC (Cicero, *Letters to Atticus* 1.6.2 = SB *A*2). Asconius or his source was probably misled by the non-chronological traditional numbering of the letters, in which this letter is found shortly after the letters from 65 BC on Cicero's election prospects.

64   Cassius is mentioned three times by Sallust as a conspirator (Sallust, *Catiline* 17.3, 44.1–2, 50.4) and by Cicero as the conspirator who wanted to burn Rome (Cicero, *Catiline* 3.14, 3.25, 4.13).

65   Julius Caesar spoke against the death-penalty being inflicted on the Catilinarian conspirators (Sallust, *Catiline* 51) and thereby incurred suspicion of having been involved. Marcus Crassus, one of the foremost and richest politicians of the time also came under vague suspicion ('At the time there were people who believed Crassus was not without knowledge of the plot.' – Sallust, *Catiline* 17).

66   *Expositio Consiliorum Suorum* – A work not published in Cicero's lifetime, and now lost, but also mentioned in several of Cicero's letters to Atticus (2.6.2, 8.1, 12.3, 14.17.6, 16.11.3) and by later historians (Dio 39.10.3 and Plutarch *Crassus* 13).

67   The so-called 'First Catilinarian Conspiracy', which most scholars now think is entirely fictitious ('one of the great red herrings of Roman history' – D.H. Berry, introduction to *in Catilinam* in *Cicero Political Speeches*, page 136).

68   As Asconius' comments make clear, the first question refers to Catiline, the second to Antonius. One duty of a patron would be to represent his clients in court. Cicero's point is that Catiline would be little good as a patron in this context. Q. Cicero makes the same point in *SGE* 8.

69   For Lucius Cornelius Sulla Felix the dictator, see footnote 19.

Tanusius.[70] In addition Marcus Marius Gratidianus, who was very much a *popularis* and therefore twice praetor, had had his head cut off by Catiline and actually carried by him through the city. Cicero frequently brings up this charge throughout the speech, since this man Gratidianus had been a close family connection of Cicero.[71]

In addition he said that Gaius Antonius could not have any clients, because he had robbed many people in Greece after gaining control of squadrons of cavalry from Sulla's army. Then the Greeks who had been robbed brought Antonius before Marcus Lucullus who was the praetor in charge of the court which had jurisdiction over provincials. Gaius Julius Caesar, then a very young man, whom we mentioned earlier, acted for the Greeks. When Lucullus passed judgement in favour of the demands of the Greeks, Antonius called the tribunes and stated on oath that he rejected the decision on the grounds that he was being denied equal rights. Six years before this speech was delivered the censors Gellius and Lentulus[72] expelled Antonius from the Senate and signed a notice giving as reasons that he had plundered allies; had rejected a court judgement; had mortgaged his estates because of huge debts and held no property in his own name.[73]

[3] Nor did he respect the Senate when he was publicly censured in his absence   85C
by your most weighty decrees.
Catiline was appointed governor of Africa directly after being praetor: after seriously damaging this province, ambassadors from Africa lodged complaints against him in the senate in his absence, and many serious criticisms were made of him in the Senate.[74]

[4] He learnt how much power was vested in the so-called courts on his so-called
acquittal.
A year prior to this speech, on his return from Africa, in the consulship of Torquatus and Cotta [65 BC], Catiline was accused of extortion by the young Publius Clodius who was later an enemy of Cicero.[75] Fenestella writes that Catiline was defended by Marcus Cicero.[76] What makes me doubt this is this very speech of Cicero, especially since he makes no mention of this matter as he could have done to create ill-feeling against an election rival for having so shamefully made an alliance against him.

---

70 Compare the slightly different list in *SGE* 9–10.

71 For Gratidianus' murder see footnote 22.

72 Lucius Gellius and Gnaeus Cornelius Lentulus Clodianus, the consuls of 72 BC were elected censors for 70 BC and carried out a thorough purge on corruption in the Senate.

73 Membership of the Senate depended on birth, election, a property qualification and good morals. One role of the censors, the most senior regularly-elected magistrates, was to review the list of eligible senators.

74 Africa at this point comprised the northern half of modern Tunisia – the promontory of Africa nearest Sicily and not very much greater in size.

75 Publius Clodius Pulcher, *c.* 92–52 BC. One of the most turbulent politicians of the late republic. From the patrician Claudius family, he made his mark as a popular firebrand politician, spelling his name in the popular way and going through the process of being adopted into a plebeian family in 59. He enjoyed the often violent support of large sections of the urban *plebs*. In 61 he was involved in a political/sexual scandal for trespassing on the women-only rites of the Bona Dea (Good Goddess) disguised as a woman. Despite Cicero giving evidence against him, Clodius was acquitted, probably by bribery. Clodius took revenge as tribune for 58 by passing legislation exiling Cicero; his thugs burned down Cicero's house. He was eventually killed in a brawl by supporters of his arch-rival for the praetorship, Milo, whose defence on a murder charge Cicero undertook (*pro Milone*).

76 Fenestella 52 BC – AD 19 wrote a history of Rome up to 57 BC. His works only survive in fragments. Though apparently reliable, he is wrong here, for the reasons suggested by Asconius. He was probably misled by Cicero's letter on defending Catiline (*Letter to Atticus* 1.2, page 11).

Especially as in this very speech, Cicero reminds his other election rival, Antonius, that it was due to his own help that Antonius had come third instead of last when a candidate for the praetorship.

[5] **Are you not aware that while I was elected as praetor in first place, you were merely added on in third place instead of last, by rivals retiring, recount of the reckoning (*centuria*), and particularly by my help?**[77]

So how can it be that someone who thinks that his electoral support for Antonius is worth mentioning, would not also think preserval of citizen rights worth mentioning if he had actually defended Catiline?[78] That this is the case is clear from what he says immediately afterwards. For Quintus Mucius Orestinus, the tribune of the people, was using his veto to prevent the law on bribery being passed, and was seen as doing this in support of Catiline. It is this man, Mucius, whom Cicero addresses in this speech in the words:

86C

[6] **But I am disgusted at you, Quintus Mucius, for thinking so little of the Roman people as to say yesterday that I am not worthy of being consul. Really? Would the Roman people have been any less careful in choosing someone to represent their interests than you were yourself? When Lucius Calenus brought an action against you for theft, you wanted me as the person best able to defend your interests.[79] So is the Roman people, at your instigation, to reject as its representative in the highest affairs of state the very same man whose advice you chose in your own disgusting affair? Unless, I suppose, you are going to claim that at the time when you did a deal with Lucius Calenus over that theft, you saw that you could not get enough help from me.**

Cicero really did take on Mucius' case, just as Fenestella wants him to be thought to have done for Catiline. But why then, although Cicero has a poor opinion of Mucius' case, does he nonetheless bring up against Mucius the fact that he had represented Mucius in court, but not do the same with Catiline if he recently spoke for Catiline? And why does he heap ridicule on Catiline's actual trial far more often than he surely would have done if he had represented him in the trial? And besides other examples, had Catiline been acquitted of extortion with Cicero representing him, it certainly seems hardly likely that he would have said:

[7] **He ruined himself by all sorts of sexual and other scandals; bloodied himself by cold-blooded murder; ripped off our allies; corrupted laws, judicial inquiries, and law-courts –**

and, later on:

[8] **What am I to say publicly of how you corrupted the province? For I dare not speak of how you behaved there since you were acquitted. Presumably then I am to assume that Roman *equites* were lying, that false statements were given by that**

87C

---

[77] It is not known whether or how Cicero really could have helped move Antonius higher up the list of elected candidates.

[78] Compare Q. Cicero, *SGE* 21, 38.

[79] Cicero describes himself here as *patronus* of Mucius – see comments on the roles of patron and client in footnote 32.

most highly-regarded community, that Quintus Metellus Pius was lying, that the province was lying: that the jurors who found you not guilty saw something (I don't know what) in your defence.[80] **You wretch, not realising that you were not really acquitted by that judgement but preserved for some harsher judgement and greater punishment!**

Is it really likely that he would make such an attack on Catiline if he had obtained his acquittal as defence counsel? Another decisive point is that although there are notes on Cicero's cases there is not a single note or summary for this one.

The way in which Catiline was acquitted damaged Clodius' reputation as having colluded: for even the objections to jurors seemed to have been carried out according to the wishes of the accused.[81]

[9] As for the people, he showed how much he cared for their opinion when, while the people looked on, he cut the neck of a real *popularis*.

We mentioned earlier that Catiline carried the head of Marius Gratidianus through the city.

[10] As for me, I cannot decide what insanity led him to insult me. Did he think I would just grin and bear it? Yet in the case of a very close connection of his, he had seen that I moved heaven and earth to punish wrongs inflicted even on other people.

Clearly Cicero means Verres.[82]

[11] The other sold all his livestock and most of his land, yet kept on his shepherds to stir up at any moment he likes, so he says, an instant war of runaway slaves.[83]

He means Gaius Antonius.

[12] The other persuaded someone in his power unexpectedly to promise to provide a public gladiator-show which was not required; the candidate for the consulship himself inspected, chose and paid for these gladiators, in full view of members of the public.

He seems to mean Quintus Gallius, whom he defended after Gallius' election against a charge of bribery. For when Gallius was a candidate to be praetor, on the grounds that he had not had animal-hunts the previous year when aedile, he put on a gladiatorial show on the pretext that he was giving it on behalf of his father.[84]

88C

---

[80] Cicero refers to evidence given in Catiline's extortion trial. The equestrians could be *publicani* or other prominent businessmen dealing with the province; Utica, capital of the province, had the privileged status of a 'free city' (*civitas libera*); Quintus Caecilius Metellus Pius was chief priest (*pontifex maximus*) 81–63 BC, distinguished politician (consul 80) and general, who had close connections with Africa having served under his father's command in the Jugurthine War (fought against Jugurtha in Numidia (= NE Algeria) 112–104 BC) and having spent time there when in exile under Cinna in 87–84 BC.

[81] This is borne out by Cicero's letter stating that the defence had the jury it wanted with the full collaboration of the prosecutor – see above, (*Letter to Atticus* 1.2, page 11).

[82] Cicero's prosecution in 70 BC of Verres, former governor of Sicily, made his reputation. Verres' only known connection with Catiline is that they both served under Sulla, but Cicero wants to establish that both were notoriously corrupt as provincial governors, and to recall his most famous case.

[83] Cicero evokes the recent Spartacus revolt (73–71 BC) finally crushed by Crassus and Pompey.

[84] Those elected aedile were expected to put on gladiatorial shows, which though costly were also a means of gaining great popular recognition (compare commercial sponsorship of modern sport) and support. For further details, see *pro Murena* 38, with notes, page 44.

[13] Therefore increase the sum you are paying to Quintus Mucius as well, if you wish, so that he may persist in blocking the law as he began blocking the decree of the Senate; I am satisfied with that law by which we saw two consuls designate condemned at one and the same time.

He means the Calpurnian law, which Gaius Calpurnius Piso had enacted three years before for bribery (*ambitus*). In his statement that the consuls designate were condemned, he means Publius Sulla and Publius Autronius, whom we have already mentioned, to be understood.[85] The full name of the tribune whom he names was Quintus Mucius Orestinus.[86]

[14] And I make no mention of his being a thug in Sulla's army; a gladiator when he entered the city; a charioteer in victory games.

It is clear that Cicero is speaking about Antonius. He calls him **a thug in Sulla's army** because of the cavalry squadrons with which we have mentioned he plagued Greece; **a gladiator when he entered the city** applies to the hated proscriptions which then took place;[87] **a charioteer in victory games,** because, when Sulla held circus games after his victory with prominent people driving chariots, Gaius Antonius was one of their number.[88]

89C   **[15] But really, Catiline, is it not astonishing and unprecedented for you to hope or think of becoming consul? Who do you think will vote for you? Our leading citizens? When advising the consul Lucius Volcacius, they did not even want you to have the right to stand for election.**

We mentioned a little earlier that Catiline turned up when he was stepping down from governing Africa to stand for the consulship and that ambassadors from the province had made serious allegations against him in the Senate. Then Catiline announced that he was standing for the consulship. Lucius Volcacius Tullus, the consul, held an official meeting to decide whether he should have to abide by Catiline's decision, if he were to stand for the consulship, since he was under investigation for extortion. For this reason Catiline gave up his candidature.[89]

[16] From the senators? They were behind your almost being stripped of all honours and handed over in chains to the spokesmen from Africa.

We have just said something about this, as a trial for extortion followed in which Catiline was scandalously acquitted, but the votes of the senators would have condemned him, while those of the *equites* and tribunes went in his favour.[90]

---

[85]   See footnote 60: these men had been elected consuls for 65 BC. It was this Sulla whom Cicero successfully defended in 62 BC on a charge of involvement in Catiline's conspiracy. Cicero was paid 2 million sesterces.

[86]   Any of the ten elected tribunes of the people had the power to veto legislation.

[87]   For proscriptions, see footnote 19.

[88]   At this time gladiators and charioteers (together with actors and prostitutes) had fewer legal rights than ordinary citizens.

[89]   Sallust, *Catiline*, 18.3 says 'Catiline was prevented from standing because he had not been able to announce his candidature within the prescribed time-limit.' Lewis plausibly suggests that Volcacius' consultation will have been on whether to allow Catiline to stand in the election re-run caused by the conviction of both consuls-designate (*Asconius*, page 297).

[90]   At this time the extortion court (*quaestio de repetundis*) comprised equal numbers of senators, equestrians and *tribuni aerarii* – a group of unclear definition, but with the same property qualification as equestrians.

[17] **From the equestrian order? You murdered them.**

The equestrian order had stood for the party of Cinna against Sulla. Many of them had embezzled money, for which they were referred to as pickpockets, and because of the hatred they had incurred they were killed after Sulla's victory.[91]

[18] **From the *plebs*? Your savagery offered them a spectacle such that no one can see you without groaning or recalling his grief.**

He attacks him for having carried about the head of Marius Gratidianus mentioned earlier. Where he said Catiline had carried about Marius' head, his words were: 90C

[19] **That head, still then full of life and breath, he brought in his own hands to Sulla, all the way from the Janiculum Hill to the Temple of Apollo.**

Everything is clear. But do not be misled by the fact that at present it is the Temple of Apollo on the Palatine Hill which is most famous:[92] you should take note that it is not this temple that Cicero means, since this was built many years after the death of Cicero by Imperator Caesar, whom we now know as the Deified Augustus, after his victory at Actium.[93] Instead he means the temple outside the Gate of Carmentis, between the Vegetable Market and the Circus of Flaminius, which was, at the time, the only Temple of Apollo in Rome.[94]

To Catiline he says:

[20] **What is there that you can say in your defence that they could not? Yet they used many arguments not possible for you.**

And a little later:[95]

[21] **In short, they could, and did, deny the charge: you have not even left yourself room shamelessly to plead 'Not Guilty'. Therefore the jurors will be said to have brought in remarkable verdicts if after convicting Luscius who pleaded 'Not Guilty' they are to acquit Catiline who admitted it.**

The Lucius Luscius whom he names was a notorious centurion of Sulla, who made a fortune from his victory – for he was worth more than 100,000 sesterces. He had been convicted not long before Cicero's speech. He was accused of the murder of three of the   91C proscribed. At about the same time, Lucius Bellienus, whom Cicero says was an uncle of Catiline, was also convicted. On the orders of Sulla, then holding the dictatorship, Bellienus had killed Lucretius Ofella, who was standing for the consulship against Sulla's wishes, to stir up civil unrest. In their cases, therefore, Cicero says it was no

---

91 Cicero obviously greatly oversimplifies and exaggerates the undoubted conflict between the two leading figures in the 80s BC, Lucius Cornelius Cinna and Lucius Cornelius Sulla Felix (see footnote 19).

92 See LACTOR 17, page 243 with further references.

93 Death of Cicero, 43 BC. The battle of Actium in 31 BC effectively ended the civil war between Octavian/Augustus and Mark Antony (and Cleopatra). In fact the temple was promised in 36 BC after the elimination of Lepidus and Sextus Pompey, two other rivals to Octavian/Augustus, and was dedicated on 9 October 28 BC. Lewis' excellent translation of Asconius oddly omits the phrase 'after his victory at Actium' (page 181).

94 This temple of Apollo is that commonly known now, and by the Elder Pliny (a younger contemporary of Asconius), as the temple of Apollo Sosianus, as a result of a rebuilding carried out by Sosius (consul for 32 BC). Three columns of this temple stand near the Theatre of Marcellus.

95 Sections 20 and 21 show Cicero accusing Catiline of murders during Sulla's proscriptions. Julius Caesar, as praetor in charge of the murder court in 64 BC had encouraged prosecution of those of Sulla's men who had killed citizens in the proscriptions. Sulla had ordered him to divorce his first wife, Cornelia, daughter of Sulla's opponent, Cinna. Caesar had refused and was probably aware that he could easily have fallen victim to the proscriptions himself.

excuse for them to claim that they were people without experience, who, if they had killed anyone would have been obeying orders from their commander and dictator, but who were able to deny the charge: Catiline, however, could not plead 'Not Guilty'. A few months later Catiline did face prosecution on the charge made by Cicero. For after the elections for consul had been held and Catiline defeated, Lucius Lucceius, a man of culture and learning, and subsequently also a candidate for the consulship, prosecuted him for murder.[96]

[22] Are you in a position to allow you to despise and look down on me, or in the one to which the rest of your life has led you? For your life has been such that there is no place so sacred that your arrival there did not result in crimes being alleged, even when unsubstantiated.
Fabia, the Vestal Virgin, had been defended on a charge of having sex, allegedly with Catiline, and had been found not guilty.[97] This Fabia was the sister of Terentia, Cicero's wife. This is why he said 'even when unsubstantiated'. In this way he spared his own family but was no less severe in charging his enemy with perversion of the most shameful kind.

[23] Whenever you were caught in adultery, whenever you yourself caught adulterers, when you found yourself a wife and daughter from the same act of sexual depravity.
92C   Catiline is said to have committed adultery with the woman who later became his mother-in-law, and to have married the product of that adultery, though she was his own daughter. Lucceius also makes this allegation about Catiline in the speeches he wrote at his prosecution. I have not yet discovered the names of these women.

[24] What am I to say publicly of how you corrupted the province, despite the protests and opposition of the whole Roman people? For I dare not speak of how you behaved there since you were acquitted.
It has quite frequently been mentioned that Catiline was appointed governor of Africa directly after being praetor, and that he was prosecuted by Publius Clodius for extortion but acquitted.[98]

[25] I make no mention of that dastardly attempt of yours which almost brought about a day of bitter grief for the state when, aided and abetted by Gnaeus Piso, not to name anyone else, you desired to carry out the massacre of the optimates.
You know the people he does not name. For there was a theory that Catiline and Gnaeus Piso, a young desperado, had conspired to carry out the massacre of the Senate, the year before this speech was given, in the consulship of Cotta and Torquatus [65 BC],

---

[96]   Lucius Lucceius, praetor in 67 BC; stood unsuccessfully for the consulship in 60; wrote a contemporary history (Cicero, *Letters to Friends* 5.12 = SB *F*22, writes asking for favourable treatment) as well as publishing his speech against Catiline (see section 23). His only writing to survive is a letter of consolation to Cicero on the death of his daughter in 45 BC (*Letters to Friends* 5.14 = SB *F*251).

[97]   The 6 Vestal Virgins formed the only female priesthood of Rome, drawn exclusively from the upper classes, responsible for keeping alight the undying flame in the Temple of Vesta, the symbolic hearth and home of Rome, and guarantee of her permanence. Priestesses found guilty of sexual relationship were executed by being buried alive.

[98]   See Asconius [4] and footnote 75.

and that this massacre was not carried out simply because Catiline had given the signal to the conspirators before they were ready.[99] Piso, however, had died by the time of this speech, having been sent to Spain by the Senate on an important embassy to get him out of the way. There he was killed while inflicting injuries on people in the provinces, as some believed, by clients of Gnaeus Pompey acting on his wishes.

[26] **Or have you forgotten that when we were candidates for the praetorship, you begged me to give up first place to you? When you did this far too frequently and pestered me far too shamelessly, do you remember my replying to you that you were acting shamelessly in begging from me what Boculus would never have got from you.**[100]   93C

We have said above that at the games which Sulla held to celebrate his victory, Gaius Antonius and certain other *nobiles* raced chariots. What is more, Antonius held the treasury contract to supply racing chariots for a fee, a contract which senators are legally able to hold. Boculus was the best-known chariot-racing driver in the Circus.

He is speaking of bad citizens:

[27] **Those who tried and failed to sever the sinews of Roman citizens with a Spanish penknife are now trying to unsheathe two blades at the same time against the state.**

The Spanish penknife is what he calls Gnaeus Piso who, as I mentioned, was killed in Spain. That Catiline and Antonius are called the two blades is obvious.

[28] **You should be aware that that 'heavy', Licinius, has already let his hair grow long because of the forthcoming trial of Catiline, as has Quintus Curius, previously a quaestor.**[101]

This Curius was very well-known as a gambler and was afterwards convicted. Calvus' elegant line of verse, 'Curius with his doctorate in dice-rolling' is about him.

Epilogue

To this speech of Cicero, both Catiline and Antonius replied with personal attacks on him being a new man, which was all they could manage. There are also speeches   94C
published in their names, though not written by them but by those denigrating Cicero: these, I suppose, are better ignored. Anyway Cicero was elected consul by all sections of the electorate: Antonius defeated Catiline by only a couple of *centuriae*, since on account of his father's reputation,[102] a slightly more respectable group campaigned for him than for Catiline.

---

[99] For the so-called 'First Catilinarian Conspiracy' see footnote 67. Further (probably invented) details, especially about Gnaeus Calpurnius Piso are given by Sallust, *Catiline*, 18–19: this may be the source for Asconius, or both may be following a common source, possibly Cicero's *Political Memoirs* – see footnote 66.

[100] The exact point of Cicero's comment is unclear, but the general purpose is clearly to stress Antonius' disreputable conduct and associates, as well as Cicero's wit.

[101] The Latin text here is damaged – I follow Lewis' suggestion that Cicero refers to the known custom of defendants appearing as if in mourning.

[102] Politician (consul in 99 BC) and distinguished lawyer, whose oratory was much admired by Cicero.

CICERO, *SECOND SPEECH TO THE PEOPLE ON THE AGRARIAN LAW AGAINST RULLUS*, 1–8

At the end of December 64, a tribune of the people, Publius Servilius Rullus, at the start of his year of office, introduced a wide-ranging agrarian bill with the aim of redistributing land in Italy and the provinces to the poor. This 'public land' (*ager publicus*) in fact tended to be leased for profitable farming to wealthy citizens. Agrarian reform had long been a source of discord within Roman society and politics, notably in the reforms of the Gracchi brothers (133–122 BC). This reform was thought to have the backing of Crassus and Caesar and to be directed against Pompey's political interests. It was clearly one which would be supported by *populares* and opposed by optimates, except those including, it seems, Gaius Antonius, Cicero's fellow consul who expected to be chosen on the ten man committee which would have unlimited powers in the redistribution of land (Plutarch, *Life of Cicero* 12.2–3). Cicero, who like most *novi homines* wanted to become part of the establishment, not abolish it, was quick to reassure the Senate from his first day as consul that he would do everything to oppose the bill (*Speeches 1 and 3 on the Agrarian Law* – both to the Senate). Yet, being an experienced politician, he was quick to reassure the people that he was really acting with their best interests at heart. Hence his pledge (sections 6–7) to be a *popularis* consul, but on his own definition. The issue of land redistribution was one exploited by Catiline in his campaign and then conspiracy later in the year, following defeat of the bill by Cicero.

[1] Usual election speeches by *nobiles*
It is an old and well-established custom, citizens, that those whom you have honoured with the consulship, and whose portrait masks may thus be placed among those of their ancestors, should in their first public speech combine an expression of their gratitude towards you for the favour you have shown them with praise of their ancestors. On these occasions it sometimes happens that a man proves himself worthy of the position attained by his ancestors, but generally all these men do is make it seem as if you have not paid in full the sum you owe their ancestors but are still in debt to their descendants.

Wax **portrait masks** (*imagines*) of ancestors who had been praetor or consul were displayed prominently in the *atrium* of a Roman house and worn at family funerals (Polybius 6.53; Pliny, *Natural History* 35.6).

Cicero's *apologia*
I cannot speak to you about my ancestors, citizens; not because they were any different from what you see me to be – I am of their blood and trained according to their principles – but because they took no part in politics and thus never enjoyed the glory and renown you can confer on a man by electing him to high office. [2] If I were to speak to you about myself, I am afraid I might seem conceited, while not to do so might seem ungrateful. For it is very difficult for me to mention myself the efforts by which I have achieved this distinction and yet I cannot possibly pass over in silence the favours you have done me. For this reason I shall adopt a strictly cautious procedure in my speech and, while I recall how much I owe you, shall discreetly venture to explain why I deserve the great esteem in which you hold me and the high office to which you have elected me, hoping that your opinion of me will remain what it has always been.

[3] The unprecedented manner of Cicero's election

I am the first *novus homo* whom you have made consul for a very long time, the first, one might almost say, within living memory. Under my leadership you have stormed the citadel which the nobility had fortified so carefully and kept under such close guard, and have shown that in future you wish its gates to stand wide open to the claims of merit. It is not simply that you have made me consul, in itself a great honour, but that you have done so in a way few *nobiles* in this city have ever become consul and, before me, no *novus homo*. Certainly, if you consider what happened to other *novi homines*, you will find that those who reached the consulship at their first attempt stood for election many years after they had been praetor, when they were well past the minimum age set by law, and that they all owed their success to continual effort and to a happy choice of the right year to stand; but those who were candidates at the minimum age were never elected on their first attempt. I am the only one of all the *novi homines* we can remember who both stood for office at the minimum age and was elected at the first attempt. These facts make it impossible for anyone to claim that the honour which I have received from you was snatched from some other candidate or won only after continual requests; I stood for the consulship at the correct point in my career, and my success must be seen as the reward of merit.

Cicero boasts about being the first member of his family to be elected to the Senate – a *novus homo*; being the first such *novus homo* to reach the consulship since 83 BC; being elected consul at the lowest permitted age (42). He uses a very similar military metaphor of having **stormed** the consulship in *pro Murena* 17, later in the same year.

[4] The voting procedure on polling day

I repeat, citizens; it is indeed a great honour that I am the first *novus homo* to become consul for many years, that I was elected in the first year in which I was a candidate, and that I was a candidate at the minimum age permitted by law; but nothing can be more glorious or splendid than the fact that, when you elected me consul, you did not do so in silence, relying on the ballot to protect your freedom of choice, but openly, raising your voices as an indication of your goodwill towards me and enthusiasm for my cause. My election as consul did not remain in doubt until all the votes were counted but was clear from the very moment you began to assemble; it was proclaimed not by the successive announcements of the various heralds but by a single unanimous shout from the entire Roman people.

The heralds announced the votes of each century. All centuries voted for Cicero, according to his *On Duties* 2.59 and this is presumably what he represents here as a **'single unanimous shout'**.

[5] The worries facing Cicero

This favour you have shown me, citizens, is exceptional, indeed unique; I recognise that it brings me considerable gratification and delight but also, and to an even greater extent, worry and concern. I am continually prey to anxieties of the most serious nature, which allow me no rest either by day or by night. Above all, I must protect the office of consul, a task difficult and worrying enough for any man, but particularly so for me. If I make a mistake, I cannot hope for pardon, and, if I succeed, I shall receive but slight and grudging praise. I cannot count upon the faithful advice of the nobility when I am uncertain what to do, nor upon their unquestioning support when I am in danger.

[6] Cicero pledges to be a *'popularis* consul'

But if the risk were mine alone, citizens, I could bear it more easily. I have the impression, though, that there are certain men who will take advantage of any mistake I may make, whether it really deserves censure or is purely accidental, to find general fault with you all for preferring me to the nobility. My object, however, must be to ensure that all my actions and all my decisions are greeted with praise for your action in deciding to elect me consul, and I consider that I should be prepared to suffer any fate rather than fail in this. What makes my task as consul even more difficult and dangerous is that I have decided that I should not follow the same rules or act on the same principles as previous holders of this office. Some of them, indeed, have gone to great lengths to avoid coming here and speaking to you face to face, while the others have done so only reluctantly. As for me, the promise I am about to make you here, where it is an easy thing to say, I have already made in the Senate where such language seemed quite out of place; as I said there in my first speech, on 1 January, I shall be a *popularis* consul.

[7] Cicero explains the dangers of the term *'popularis'*

I realise that I owe my election, in which I far outstripped men of the highest nobility, not to the support of a group of powerful men nor to the far-reaching influence of a small minority, but to the will of the entire Roman people. It is inevitable, then, that both now in my year of office and throughout the rest of my life I shall be seen to be on the side of the people. But in attempting to explain the true force and meaning of this phrase 'a *popularis* consul' I stand in great need of your understanding, for a dangerously misleading impression of its meaning is now becoming current, caused by the hypocritical claims of a group of men who attack and frustrate the true interests and well-being of the people while making it the object of their speeches to win a reputation as *populares*.

Cicero sets out his aim, accomplished in the rest of his speech, of persuading the people that Rullus' law, though about land redistribution, that most *popularis* of all measures, would actually work against their best interests. Thus he opposes the law, not as an optimate, but as a truer *popularis* than Rullus. This paradoxical and disingenuous argument was plausible because of his status as a *novus homo* and not therefore one of the traditional senatorial elite and because of his recent election. It does not mean that he was elected as a *popularis* (see, for example *SGE* 5); nor, for that matter, does it mean he was an optimate.

[8] Threats to the state

The state for which I assumed responsibility on 1 January was, I know, deeply affected by terror and anxiety. There was no limit to the fears of respectable men, nor to the confident expectations of the wicked; every sort of disaster and calamity was considered possible. It was reported that all kinds of revolutionary plots against the present form of government and against the freedom you now enjoy were either being started or had been in progress from the time when I became consul designate. There was no feeling of confidence in public life, but its loss was due not to some sudden crushing disaster but to suspicion, to disorder in the law courts and to the invalidating of decisions already reached in them. There was a general feeling that the aim behind all this was the re-establishment of dictatorial power in some new form, that these men would not be satisfied with constitutional authority, on however grand a scale, but were bent on tyranny.

Politicians more recent than Cicero have, of course, been suspected of doing what Cicero does here in using unspecified reports of serious plots by unnamed groups as a means of persuading the public to support his policies.

CICERO, SPEECH IN DEFENCE OF MURENA

As consul, Cicero presided over the elections for the next pair of consuls. These were hotly contested. Catiline, prevented from standing in previous years, and then defeated by Cicero, stood once again. So too did another of the defeated candidates for 63, Decimus Iunius Silanus, and two other candidates standing at their earliest available opportunity, Lucius Licinius **Murena** and Servius **Sulpicius** Rufus. Cicero managed to prevent Catiline's election by allowing Lucius Licinius **Lucullus** a long-delayed triumph. This meant that Lucullus' troops were in Rome for the election, and they duly voted for Murena who, like his father before him, had served under Lucullus. It was this latest electoral rebuff which seems to have prompted Catiline to turn to conspiracy. However the election campaign had also been marked by an unusually high level of bribery. Sulpicius Rufus thus prosecuted his rival Murena: if successful, he would take Murena's place. Cicero though a friend of Sulpicius' defended Murena. He does not answer the bribery charge (Murena was presumably as guilty as most Roman politicians) but instead makes the point that Murena's election as *novus homo* ahead of the patrician Sulpicius was not proof of bribery. He also shows that in practical terms, Rome needs a soldier's sword not a lawyer's quibbles to deal with the threat of Catiline.

The selection below is not intended to be representative of the speech as a whole, but highlights the parts where Cicero can, in the context of his defence of Murena, suggest factors possibly thought of as relevant in consular campaigns. Throughout these selections, Cicero contrasts his client, Murena, with the main prosecutor, the lawyer and defeated candidate, Servius Sulpicius Rufus. Cicero does not exaggerate their friendship outside this court case, which presumably made Cicero's defence more effective, but also more offensive for Sulpicius. See, for example, Sulpicius' letter of consolation to Cicero on the death of his daughter (*Letters to Friends* 4.5 = SB F248) and Cicero's 'eulogy' on Sulpicius (Cicero, *Philippic* 9, especially 9.10–12) asking the Senate to grant him a public funeral: a different and surely more accurate picture.

Pro Murena 21–25
[21] Questionable advantage of being always in the Forum
Each of them is a man of the greatest distinction and the greatest merit (*dignitas*); and if Servius allowed me to, I would judge their merits equal and worthy of the same praise. But no, he attacks the military life, lays into the whole of Murena's service as legate, and thinks that the consulship is a matter only of one's constant presence in the Forum and a succession of daily legal tasks. "Do you mean to tell me that you've been with the army," say he, "and haven't been near the Forum for so many years? And when after this prolonged absence you finally appear, are you to compete for position with those who have made the Forum their home?" To begin with, Servius, this continuous presence of ours: you don't realise how men can sometimes have too much of it, become bored by it. Certainly it stood me in excellent stead that my popularity was before the eyes of all; but it was only by great efforts on my part that I overcame men's boredom with me, and, I dare say, you have done so too; all the same, it would have been no bad thing for either of us if men had felt our absence.

Of course, when the case demanded it, Cicero could make the opposite point that he could not be too often seen in the Forum – *pro Plancio* 66, and we need not doubt that he genuinely missed being in the public eye in his (mandatory) year as governor of Cilicia (*Letters to Atticus* 5.15.1 = SB A108). Compare also his advice from Cilicia to the aedile Caelius Rufus – 'The city, the city, my dear Rufus, stay in it and live in its limelight.' – *Letters to Friends* 2.12 = SB F95.

[22] Relative glories of military, compared with legal, experience

If I may leave this aside, however, and return to the comparison of your respective callings and skills, how can there be any doubt that, when it comes to getting the consulship, the glory of a military career produces far greater distinction (*dignitas*) than the glory which comes from civil law? You get up long before dawn to prepare opinions for your clients; he does so, in order to reach his destination with his army in good time. You are woken by the cock's crow, he by the sound of the bugle; you draw up a case, he draws up a line of battle. You guard against your clients being convicted, he against cities or camps being captured; he uses his skill and knowledge to keep off the forces of the enemy, you to keep out rainwater. He is well practised in extending boundaries, you in delimiting them. Small wonder, indeed, – for I must express what I feel – that excellence in the art of war outshines all other virtues. It is this that has won for the Roman people its name, and for our city imperishable glory; it is this that has compelled the world to acknowledge our sway; all our business in the city, all these precious occupations of ours, our fame at the bar, our hard work, lie safe under the protection and defence of martial valour. The moment a hint of war makes itself heard, our skills fall silent at once.

[23] Legal knowledge no guarantee of a consulship

Now as you appear to me to be caressing this legal knowledge of yours as though it were your dear little daughter, I do not propose to let you linger under such a delusion as to think that this thing – whatever it is – that you have so laboriously learned is really anything very special. Because of your other qualities – your self-control, your dignity, your sense of justice, your honesty – I have always considered you fully deserving of the consulship, and indeed of every distinction; but as for your mastery of the civil law, I will not call it wasted labour, but I will say that there is no beaten path to the consulship in that field of study. All such professions as serve to win us the support of the Roman people ought to possess an intrinsic merit (*dignitas*) that men can admire and a usefulness that earns great popularity.

[24] Greatest *dignitas* in the military

The highest merit (*dignitas*) resides in those who have won outstanding glory in war; everything in the empire, every element in our constitution, is, we believe, defended and strengthened by them; they are also the most useful, if it is indeed true that by their advice and by the dangers they undergo, we are enabled to enjoy not only our political life but also our very property. Another thing that is important and of great worth (*dignitas*) is the power of eloquent speech, a thing which has often proved decisive in the election of a consul – the power to sway the hearts of Senate, people or jury by reasoned oratory. We are looking for a consul who by his oratory can sometimes check the frenzied agitations of the tribunes, appease the excitement of the people, and stand out against bribery. It is not surprising if men who were often not even *nobiles* have achieved the consulship by this power of theirs, particularly when at the same time it earns them the widest popularity, the most steady *amicitiae*, and the most solid support. But none of this is true of that trade of yours, Sulpicius.

[25] Lawyers exposed

First, such a trifling subject can possess no intrinsic worth (*dignitas*): its matter is insignificant, being virtually taken up with individual letters and word-divisions.

Secondly, even if your calling did possess something that aroused the admiration of
our forefathers, this has come utterly into contempt now your mystic arts have been
divulged. Once upon a time, only a few men knew whether or not legal proceedings
could be taken: for the official calendar was not public property. Those who were
consulted on legal matters were in a very powerful position: men would actually ask
them for the right day, as if they were astrologers! But then a clerk, one Gnaeus
Flavius, was found, a man who could out-smart the smartest, and, by learning off the
individual days, he published the calendar, and filched their knowledge from under
the very noses of these canny lawyers. This made them angry, and they were afraid
that now the list of days was published and understood men could go to law without
their help: they therefore concocted some legal formulae to enable them to have a
finger in every pie.

In the sections above Cicero is not being merely hypocritical or self-effacing. Even today, despite various
reforms of the British legal profession, barristers (who act as advocates in court) do not like to be confused
with solicitors (who basically don't). Note: US terminology is completely different! It suits Cicero's case
to portray Sulpicius as a mere solicitor not a barrister, concerned with keeping out rainwater, not the enemy
(section 22). Cicero's joke works because it seems that rainwater was a problem. Ulpian's *Digest of Roman
Law* 39.3.3.1–4 contains comments on various judicial opinions concerning rainwater. In contrast Cicero is
surely thinking of himself as the sort of orator who can check the frenzied agitations of a tribune (section
24) after his successful opposition to Rullus' agrarian bill (see above, page 39). Cicero makes the obvious
points about the relative importance of military rather than civilian life (at the time of Murena's trial,
Catiline had joined forces with the rebel army of Manlius).

Pro Murena 37–38
[37] Two factors in elections to praetorship and consulship
But if I were forced to give a reason, there were two things obviously lacking in his
campaign for the praetorship both of which Murena used greatly to his advantage for
the consulship. The first was the expectation of gladiatorial shows which had grown
as a result of a great deal of gossip not to mention the partisan talk of his election
rivals. The second was that the people who had seen at first hand his generosity and
courage in the province and throughout his military command had not yet returned
home. Fortune kept back both of these to boost his consulship campaign. For the
army of Lucius Lucullus which had assembled for his triumph was also at hand for
Lucius Murena at the election, and the most magnificent gladiatorial show which his
campaign for praetor had lacked, he provided when actually praetor.

[38] The military vote matters
Do you think that only a small amount of help and support in gaining the consulship is
represented by the backing of the soldiers, which has a weight through sheer numbers,
through their influence with their friends, and especially through the great influence
with the whole populace of Rome in electing a consul? Of course not! Commanders
are being chosen at consular elections, not interpreters of meaning. Therefore these
sorts of statements matter: "He saved me when I was wounded; he gave me a share of
the spoil; he was our leader when we captured the camp and closed with the enemy;
never did he require a soldier to take a tougher job than he was doing himself; he was
brave and also lucky." How much do you think this is worth in terms of reputation and
backing from people? And furthermore, if religious feeling at elections is so great that

the first results have always had the force of an omen, why should we be surprised that Murena's reputation for good luck and gossip about it has had a similar effect?

Games matter too

But if you think that these important matters are fairly trivial, and if you think the votes of civilians are more important than those of soldiers, do not regard with such total contempt the sophistication of his games or the grandeur of his show: these helped him significantly. What am I to say about the great delight of the people and the ignorant hordes for games? No great surprise there. But there my case rests: elections are decided by the people and the masses. Therefore, if the grandeur of the games brings such pleasure for the people, it is no surprise that it brought an advantage to Murena in the popular vote.

Military vote: Lucius Licinius **Lucullus** had claimed a triumph for defeating Tigranes, king of Armenia in 66 BC, but lost popular support and was replaced as commander by Pompey. On his return home his enemies had successfully delayed the celebration of his triumph. Murena had served as Lucullus' legate, as had his father before him: Cicero exaggerates their achievements in sections 11–12, 20, 31–4. Cicero as consul ensured the triumph took place, which meant that Lucullus' troops were in Rome for the election, and, apparently, duly voted for Murena.

Games: Certain elected magistrates at Rome (and in Italian towns) were expected to put on gladiatorial shows or pay for other civic amenities at their own expense. 'In reality, buying cheaply things of the highest value' – as Plutarch describes the huge debts incurred by Julius Caesar for his gladiatorial shows as aedile in 65 BC and the popularity this gained him (*Life of Caesar* 5.4; also Pliny, *Natural History* 33.53; Dio 37.8; Suetonius, *Julius Caesar* 10.) At Pompeii, election propaganda for candidates for senior magistrates sometimes mention shows given by the candidate when junior magistrate. Murena had not been aedile, one of the posts to require games, so did not have this advantage in seeking to be praetor, but as city praetor he did (see section 41). Legislation to limit such games was enacted in 67 BC, with provision of free seats at shows to people not in the candidate's own tribe specifically outlawed by Cicero's own amendments in 63 BC (see *pro Murena* 67).

Pro Murena 41–44

[41] The importance of the praetor's year in office in a role chosen by lot

Do you think there was no difference between the praetor's jobs allotted to him and to you? The draw gave him what all of us who were your close friends wished for you: civil jurisdiction. In this sphere the importance of the business brings prestige, the dispensing of justice, gratitude. The wise sort of praetor that Murena was, in this post, avoids causing offense by the even-handedness of his decision-making, and gains goodwill by hearing cases sympathetically. It is an excellent posting, suitable for someone aiming for the consulship, in which praise for fairness, integrity, and friendliness can lastly be rounded off with delight at the games put on. [42] What was your lot? The depressing and grim embezzlement court... (*Cicaro gives some further description of this role.*)

[42] Murena uses his post as propraetor to advantage

Finally you declined to go to a province. I cannot blame you for doing what I myself did as praetor and consul. Nonetheless his province brought Murena many genuine debts of gratitude and an excellent reputation. On his way he enlisted soldiers in Umbria. The public interest gave him the opportunity of showing a generosity through which he attached the many voting-tribes which are comprised of the *municipia* of Umbria. By his own even-handedness and perseverance in Gaul he himself saw to it that our men could settle accounts already written off. Meanwhile you were in Rome, no doubt a great comfort to your friends. How could I deny it? But perhaps consider that in some cases warmth of *amici* tends to cool towards those whom they see holding themselves aloof from provinces.

Being praetor:
Eight praetors were elected at this period. They were elected in order, but drew lots to decide which particular role each would fulfil for the year, though these overlapped. The oldest, most prominent office with precedence was that of urban praetor, who was also responsible for the annual Games of Apollo. Other praetors presided over courts dealing with various specific charges, such as embezzlement, bribery, extortion, homicide.

After their year in office, praetors again drew lots to decide which **province** they would govern as promagistrates (Cicero, *Letters to Atticus* 1.13.5, 1.14.5, 1.15.1 – 61 BC (= SB A13–15), when the lottery was delayed until early March). Cicero declined to govern a province after his praetorship, as was permissible until Pompey's reforms of 52 BC (Cicero, *Letters to Friends* 8.8.8 = SB F84), and also after his consulship, but most welcomed the opportunities offered for power, prestige, military glory and, of course, financial gain. Even Cicero when later compelled to govern Cilicia in 51/0 BC revelled in his military successes (*Letters to Friends* 2.10, 15.4, 15.10, 15.13, 16.11.3 (= SB F108–110, 143); *to Atticus* 5.20, 6.3.3 (= SB A113, 117). For potentially huge financial profits, legal or illegal, from helping provincials and *publicani*, as Murena apparently did, see *Letters to Atticus* 5.16, 5.21.7–13, 6.1, 6.2.5 (= SB 109, 114–6). *Letters to Friends* 5.20.9 (= SB F128) shows that Cicero legally obtained 2.2 million sesterces as governor. Close friends and supporters might expect a share in these too; see, for example a letter from Caelius to Cicero in Cilicia (*Letters to Friends* 8.9, Sept. 51 BC = SB F82) asking for panthers for his games and tax-exemptions for a friend.

[43] Sulpicius' mistake in threatening to prosecute during the campaign
And since I have shown, gentlemen of the jury, that Murena and Sulpicius were, in standing for the consulship, equal in their own worthiness, though not equal in their good luck with regard to provincial matters, I shall now say more explicitly in what respect my very good friend, Servius, was the weaker candidate. And I shall say in your hearing, now it is too late, exactly what I often said to him in private in good time. I frequently told you, Servius, that you did not know how to campaign for the consulship: I was always telling you that in those very areas where I saw you acting and speaking with courage and determination, you seemed to me more like a determined prosecutor than a savvy candidate. Firstly the warnings and threats of prosecution which you began to employ daily are the mark of a determined man, but turn public opinion away from expecting you to gain office and weaken support from your *amici*. It somehow always happens – I don't know how, but it has been noticed not once or twice but on many occasions – that as soon as a candidate seems to be considering a prosecution, he is seen to have given up hope of gaining office.

[44] How Cicero thinks a candidate should campaign
What then? Am I against an injured party pursuing a claim? Of course I am not. But there is a time for pursuing a claim and a time for running a campaign. I want a candidate for the consulship in particular to come down to the Forum and Field of Mars with great hopes, great enthusiasm, great crowds. I don't like one candidate collecting evidence about another (and advertising in advance his own defeat), compiling lists of witnesses instead of voters, using threats more than flattery, issuing injunctions rather than going around meeting people. Especially since just recently practically everyone goes round to the house of each candidate, guessing from the expression of each candidate how much confidence and chance of winning each seems to have.

[45] Avoid looking beaten

"Do you see him looking depressed and demoralised? He's down, he's given up, he's thrown in the towel." The rumour spreads. "Do you know he's thinking of prosecuting, investigating his election rivals, looking for witnesses. Vote for someone else, he's not got a hope." Close *amici* of the candidates are weakened by rumours of this kind and lose enthusiasm. They either give up the campaign as a foregone conclusion or save their efforts or favours for the trial and prosecution.

Cicero won his case – unanimously if we take literally his claim in *pro Flacco* 98.

BIBLIOGRAPHY

TEXTS and TRANSLATIONS

Cicero's letters: (NB some letters are actually letters *to* Cicero, written *by* others.) This area is dominated by the great D.R. Shackleton Bailey, with his own numbering system (here abbreviated to SB followed by A, F, Q for letters to Atticus, Friends and Quintus respectively). His texts, translations and commentaries can variously be found in the Cambridge Classical Texts and Commentaries series; in the old (1965/1978), three-volume Penguin series, now reduced to a selection only (1986); and in the Loeb Classical Library (8 volumes).

The last volume of the Loeb letters also contains the **Short Guide to Electioneering – *Commentariolum Petitionis*** (text and translation). Jeffrey Tatum is in the process of writing a commentary with text & translation of this text for Oxford University Press.

Asconius on Cicero *In Toga Candida* is most easily available in the excellent *Asconius: Commentaries on Speeches of Cicero*, by R.G. Lewis, Clarendon Ancient History Series, OUP 2006. This includes Latin text, excellent translation and commentary on the translation.

Cicero *pro Murena* is in *Cicero Defence Speeches* translated by D.H. Berry for Oxford World's Classics (2000).

Cicero *de lege agraria* is in the Loeb Classical Library.

Electronic Latin texts of the works by Cicero and Asconius can be found in *The Latin Library* at Ad Fontes Academy (Asconius under 'Miscellany'). The Perseus website contains Latin texts of Cicero and *Commentariolum Petitionis* with outdated translations.

STANDARD WORKS OF REFERENCE

Cambridge Ancient History, (CAH) Volume IX, 2nd edition, *The Last Age of the Roman Republic,* 146–43 BC, eds Crook, J.A., Lintott, A., Rawson, E., CUP 1994
The Oxford Classical Dictionary (OCD) 3rd edition (1996), eds Hornblower, S., & Spawforth, A.
Oxford Latin Dictionary (OLD), ed. Glare, P.G.W., (1968)

SECONDARY READING

Beard, M. & Crawford, M.H., *Rome in the Late Republic,* Duckworth 2000

Brunt, P.A., *The Fall of the Roman Republic*, OUP 1988

Crawford, M.H, *The Roman Republic*, Fontana 1978, 1992

Flower, H. (ed.), *The Cambridge Companion to the Roman Republic,* CUP 2004

Gruen, E.S., *The Last Generation of the Roman Republic*, California UP 1974

Habicht, C., *Cicero the Politician*, John Hopkins UP, 1989.

Lintott, A., *The Constitution of the Roman Republic*, OUP 1999

Lintott, A., *Cicero as Evidence, A Historian's Companion*, OUP 2008

Millar, F.G.B., *The Crowd in Rome in the Late Republic,* Ann Arbor, 1998

Morstein-Marx, R. 'Publicity, Popularity and Patronage in the Commentariolum Petitionis', *Classical Antiquity 17* (1998) 259–88.

Morstein-Marx, R., *Mass Oratory and Political Power in the Late Roman Republic,* CUP 2003

Mouritsen, H., *Plebs and Politics in the Late Roman Republic*, CUP 2001

Patterson, J.R., *Political Life in the City of* Rome, BCP 2000

Powell, J. & Paterson, J. (eds) *Cicero the Advocate*, OUP 2004

Rosenstein, N. & Morstein-Marx, R. (eds) *A Companion to the Roman Republic,* Blackwell 2006

Steel, C., *Reading Cicero: Genre and Performance in Late Republican Rome,* Duckworth 2005

Tatum, W.J., '*Alterum est tamen boni viri, alterum boni petitoris*: The Good Man Canvasses', *Phoenix* 61 no. 1–2, 2007, 109–135

Treggiari, S., LACTOR 10 (2nd ed.) *Cicero's Cilician Letters,* 1996

Wiedemann, T., *Cicero and the End of the Roman Republic*, BCP 1998

Wiseman, T.P., *New Men in the Roman Senate*, OUP 1971

Wiseman, T.P., *Remembering the Roman People*, OUP 2009

Yakobson, A., *Elections and Electioneering in Rome. A Study in the Political System of the Late Republic*, Stuttgart 1999

INDEX OF NAMES

Antonius, (Gaius Antonius – consul 63 BC)
Atticus 1.1.1; *SGE* 8, 9, 28; Asconius *Title, Pref.,* 1, 2, 4, 5, 11, 14, 20, 26, 27, *Ep.*
Notorious for profiteering from civil unrest in the 80s; expelled from the Senate in 70; re-entered the Senate through his election as praetor in 66. Elected alongside Cicero as consul for 63. Uncle of Mark Antony.

Aquilius
Atticus 1.1.1
Lawyer, mentioned as a possible rival for the consulship, but did not stand.

Aufidius
Atticus 1.1.1
Mentioned as not a serious rival for Cicero: but did not stand.

Caecilius, (Quintus Caecilius)
Asconius 2, *SGE* 9
Allegedly murdered by Catiline in Sulla's proscriptions.

Caecilius, (Quintus Caecilius)
Atticus 1.1.3–4
Uncle of Atticus, Cicero declined to represent him against Satyrus.

Caesar, (Gaius Julius Caesar – the *dictator*)
Asconius *Pref.,* 1, 2; footnote 89
Later the *dictator*. At the time of Cicero's consulship, he was well known for giving spectacular games as aedile in 65 BC, but still a fairly junior member of the Senate.

Caesar, (Lucius Julius Caesar – consul 64 BC)
Atticus 1.1.2; 1.2.1
Mentioned by Cicero as certain to be consul for 64 BC, and duly elected. His father and the aunt of Julius Caesar the Dictator were cousins.

Caesonius
Atticus 1.1.1
Mentioned as an unlikely consulship rival for Cicero: did not stand.

Cassius, (Lucius Cassius Longinus)
SGE 7; Asconius *Pref.*, footnote 64
Candidate for the consulship of 63 BC, though not, apparently, a serious rival.

Catiline, (Lucius Sergius Catilina).
Atticus 1.1.1; 1.2.1; *SGE* 8, 9; Asconius *throughout*
Of upper-class (patrician) but not recently-distinguished family. Praetor in 68, governor of Africa 67–66, he was prosecuted for extortion and thus prevented from standing for the consulships of 65 or 64. Acquitted with the connivance of his prosecutor, his defeats in the two following years led to his conspiracy.

Cincius
Atticus 1.1.1
An agent of Atticus, frequently mentioned in Cicero's letters to Atticus.

Clodius, (Publius Clodius Pulcher)
Asconius 4, 8, 24; also note on *Atticus* 1.2.1; footnote 75
92–52 BC. One of the most turbulent politicians of the late republic. From patrician Claudian family, he made his mark as a popular firebrand politician.

Coelius, (Gaius Coelius Caldus – consul 94 BC)
SGE 11, footnote 27
Coelius was the penultimate *novus homo* to become consul before Cicero.

Cornelius, (Gaius Cornelius – tribune of the people, 66 BC)
SGE 19, 51, and footnote 57; Asconius *title*
Popular tribune, defended by Cicero on a charge of treason in 65 BC.

Cornificius, Quintus:
Atticus 1.1.1; Asconius *Pref.*
Candidate for the consulship of 63 BC, though not, apparently, a serious rival.

Cotta, (Gaius Aurelius Cotta – consul 75 BC)
SGE 47
Distinguished orator (see footnote 55), from one of the most distinguished families of the generation.

Cotta, (Lucius Aurelius Cotta – consul 65 BC)
Asconius 1, 4
Brother of Gaius, who was consul 10 years before him. A third brother was consul in 73 BC.

Crassus, (Marcus Licinius Crassus – consul 70 BC)
Asconius *Pref.*, 1, footnote 65
One of the foremost and richest politicians of the time.

Domitius, (Lucius Domitius Ahenobarbus – consul 54 BC)
Atticus 1.1.3–4 (and note on 1.1.4)
Member of a leading aristocratic family. Key supporter of Cicero.

Figulus, (Gaius Marcius Figulus – consul 64 BC)
Atticus 1.2.1
Almost certainly the same person known as Thermus by Cicero in *Att* 1.1.2, the new name resulting from adoption, very common among Roman upper classes, even for adults.

Galba, (Publius Sulpicius Galba)
Atticus 1.1.1; *SGE* 7; Asc *Pref.*
Patrician (upper-class) candidate for the consulship of 63 BC.

Gallius, Quintus (praetor 65 BC)
SGE 19; Asconius 12
Defended by Cicero on a charge of election bribery in 64 BC.

Gratidianus, (Marcus Marius Gratidianus – praetor 85 BC)
SGE 10; Asconius 2, 9, 18
Twice praetor. Relative of Marius, killed by Catiline in the proscriptions.

Lucullus (Lucius Licinius Lucullus – consul 74 BC)
Atticus 1.1.3; *pro Murena* 37
Prominent politician and military commander.

Manilius, Gaius (*tribunus plebis* 66 BC)
SGE 51
Tribune of the people in 66 BC, supporter of Pompey, defended by Cicero in 65 BC.

Mucius (Quintus Mucius Orestinus, *tribunus plebis* 66 BC)
Asconius *Pref.*, 5, 6, 13
Supporter of Catiline, though previously represented by Cicero.

Palicanus: (Marcus Lollius Palicanus, *tribunus plebis* 71 BC)
Atticus 1.1.1
Popular politician and agitator, tribune in 71 BC. Piso, consul in 67 had prevented his standing for the consulship of 66.

Panthera
SGE 8
An obscure friend of Antonius.

Piso: (Gaius Calpurnius Piso, consul 67 BC)
Atticus 1.1.2; Asconius 13
Prominent aristocratic politician. As consul in 67 he introduced a law against election bribery. From 66 BC, governor of Transalpine and Cisalpine Gaul (modern SE France and Italy north of the River Po).

Piso: (Gnaeus Calpurnius Piso)
Asconius 1, 25, 27
Same family, but uncertain relationship to the above. Sent by Senate to Spain and killed there in 64 BC.

Pompey (the Great): (Gnaeus Pompeius Magnus, 106–48 BC, consul 70 BC, 55BC, 52 BC)
Atticus 1.1.2; *SGE* 5, 14, 51; Asconius 25
The most prominent politician and general of the time. From 66–62 in special command against Rome's chief enemy Mithradates in Asia (modern Turkey). Until the late 60s a *popularis*, by his return to Rome in 62 he had abandoned this position.

Sabidius
SGE 8;
An obscure friend of Antonius.

Sacerdos (Lucius Licinius Sacerdos)
Asconius *Pref.*
Rival of Cicero for the consulship of 63 BC.

Satyrus, Caninius
Atticus 1.1.3–4
Friend and supporter of Cicero.

Silanus, (Marcus Junius Silanus, consul 62 BC)
Atticus 1.1.2
Missed out in the consular election for 64 but elected for 62.

Sulla, (Lucius Cornelius Sulla Felix, consul 88 BC, dictator 82/1 BC)
SGE 9; Asconius 2, 14, 17, 19, 21, 26.
The most powerful and controversial politician in the 80s BC. Dictator and author of
the proscriptions – See footnote 19.

Publius **Sulla,** (Publius Cornelius Sulla)
Asconius 13
Nephew of the *dictator*. Elected consul for 65 BC, but convicted of bribery and
disqualified. Later accused of involvement in Catiline's conspiracy, but defended by
Cicero.

Terentia
Atticus 1.2.1; Asconius 22:
Wife of Cicero.

Turius
Atticus 1.1.2
An unsuccessful candidate for the consular elections for 64 BC.

TIMELINE OF MAJOR EVENTS IN CICERO'S LIFE AND LIST OF CONSULS 79–62 BC

Names of magistrates are printed according to their status, according to the categories set out by Asconius, *Preface*:

> **<u>patricians</u>**
> **nobiles (with recent consular ancestors)**
> *'merely not novi homines' (i.e. senatorial, but not consular ancestor(s))*
> novus homo (only Cicero)

106	Cicero born on 3 January
82	**<u>L. Cornelius Sulla</u>** *dictator*; proscriptions; various reforms
81	**<u>Sulla</u>** resigns as *dictator* (end of year)
79	consuls: **P. Servilius Vatia** & **<u>Ap. Claudius Pulcher</u>**
78	consuls: **<u>M. Aemilius Lepidus</u>** & **Q. Lutatius Catulus**
77	consuls: **D. Iunius Brutus** & **<u>Mam. Aemilius Lepidus</u>**
76	consuls: **Cn. Octavius** & *C. Scribonius Curio*
75	consuls: **L. Octavius** & **C. Aurelius Cotta**
	Cicero quaestor, and so from then on, member of the Senate
74	consuls: **L. Licinius Lucullus** & **M. Aurelius Cotta**
73	consuls: **M. Terentius Varro Lucullus** & **C. Cassius Longinus**
72	consuls: *L. Gellius* & **<u>Cn. Cornelius Lentulus Clodianus</u>**
71	consuls: **<u>P. Cornelius Lentulus Sura</u>** & *Cn. Aufidius Orestes*
70	consuls: **Cn. Pompeius (Magnus)** & **M. Licinius Crassus**
	Cicero's speeches *Against Verres*
69	consuls: **Q. Hortensius Hortalus** & **Q. Caecilius Metellus (Creticus)**
68	consuls: **L. Caecilius Metellus Pius** & **Q. Marcius Rex**
67	consuls: **C. Calpurnius Piso** & **M'. Acilius Glabrio**
66	consuls: **<u>M'. Aemilius Lepidus</u>** & *L. Volcatius Tullus*
	Cicero praetor; Cicero's speech *On Command of Pompey*
65	consuls: **L. Aurelius Cotta** & **<u>L. Manlius Torquatus</u>**
July	Cicero's *Lettters to Atticus* 1.1 and 1.2 on his prospects
64	consuls: **<u>L. Iulius Caesar</u>** & **C. Marcius Figulus**
July?	Cicero elected consul for 63 BC
63	consuls: M. Tullius Cicero & **C. Antonius**
Jan	Cicero's speeches *On the Agrarian Law*
Oct–Dec	Cicero acts against the Catilinarian conspiracy
Nov end	Cicero *pro Murena*
62	consuls: **D. Iunius Silanus** & *L. Licinius Murena*
	Defeat and death of **<u>Catiline</u>** (January)
58	Cicero exiled
57	Cicero recalled
51	Cicero governor of Cilicia
44	Assassination of **<u>Julius Caesar</u>**, *dictator*
43	Triumvirate of **Antony**, **<u>Lepidus</u>** & *Octavian* (*Augustus*) formed.
	Cicero murdered in subsequent proscriptions

Printed in the United States
by Baker & Taylor Publisher Services

Printed in the United States
by Baker & Taylor Publisher Services